THE STORY OF CANADA

JANET LUNN • CHRISTOPHER MOORE
Illustrated by ALAN DANIEL

SCHOLASTIC CANADA LTD.
New York Toronto London Auckland Sydney
Mexico City New Delhi Hong Kong Buenos Aires

For Elizabeth, Liam, Kieran, and Joe
– born during the writing of *The Story of Canada*

Scholastic Canada Ltd.
604 King Street West, Toronto, Ontario M5V 1E1, Canada

Scholastic Inc.
557 Broadway, New York, NY 10012, USA

Scholastic Australia Pty Limited
PO Box 579, Gosford, NSW 2250, Australia

Scholastic New Zealand Limited
Private Bag 94407, Greenmount, Auckland, New Zealand

Scholastic Children's Books
Euston House, 24 Eversholt Street, London NW1 1DB, UK

Library and Archives Canada Cataloguing in Publication

Lunn, Janet, 1928-
The story of Canada : a century of change / Janet
Lunn, Christopher Moore ; illustrated by Alan Daniel.
Previously published as part of : The story of
Canada. Toronto : Key Porter Books, 2007.
Includes bibliographical references and index.
ISBN 978-0-545-99618-1
1. Canada--History--1867- --Juvenile literature.
2. Canada--Biography--Juvenile literature.
I. Moore, Christopher, 1950- II. Daniel, Alan, 1939- III. Title.
FC172.L853 2009   j971.06   C2009-904113-8

Text copyright © 1992, 1996, 2000, 2007, Janet Lunn and
Christopher Moore
Original illustrations copyright © 1992 Alan Daniel unless otherwise credited

First published by Key Porter Books Limited in 1992
This edition published by Scholastic Canada Ltd. in 2009

Care has been taken to trace ownership of copyright material contained
in this book. The publishers will gladly receive any information that will enable them to
rectify any reference or credit line in subsequent editions.
See pp. 107 for full picture credits.

All rights reserved.
No part of this publication may be reproduced or stored in a retrieval system, or transmit-
ted in any form or by any means, electronic, mechanical, recording, or otherwise, without
written permission of the publisher. In the case of photocopying or other reprographic
copying, a licence must be obtained from Access Copyright (Canadian Copyright
Licensing Agency), 1 Yonge Street, Suite 800, Toronto, Ontario M5E 1E5 (1-800-893-5777).

6 5 4 3 2 1   Printed in Canada   09 10 11 12 13

Previous page: A newsboy, about 1900. Opposite: The Young Reader.
NGC/© Ozias Leduc 1992/VIS*ART.

To the Reader

We have called this book
The Story of Canada,
but we know no book has
room for all the stories of
Canada. We hope you find
something of yourself in the
tales we have told – and go
on to discover more stories
of Canada for yourself.

The Authors

Contents

Chapter 1
Stormy Times

W

Mr. Gus Gabert and his students in Bruderheim, Alberta, in 1915. During the First World War, many towns with German-sounding names changed them, but Bruderheim never did.

Previous page
At the end of the First World War, hundreds of thousands of Canadians came home. They were welcomed by big-city parades and, like this soldier at a small-town station, by their wives and children – children who sometimes barely knew their father.

AR CLOUDS GATHERED IN EUROPE IN THE SUMMER OF 1914, BUT Canadians were not very concerned about the rumble of that far-away storm. The prime minister, Sir Robert Borden, had gone away to his summer home to play golf. Across the country, boys and girls were going to summer camp with the Boy Scouts or the Girl Guides, new movements which had recently become popular. In Carlstadt, Alberta, known as "the star of the Prairies," farmers spent the summer of 1914 praying for rain. They even hired rainmakers, who roamed the dry plains of southeastern Alberta with mysterious instruments, promising to create downpours on demand.

No rain came to Carlstadt, but war came to Europe. In a town called Sarajevo, an assassin shot Franz Ferdinand, the archduke of Austria-Hungary. Tensions between the states of Europe had been building for years, and they had bound themselves together in tangled alliances. When Austria-Hungary declared war on Serbia, blaming it for the killing, the alliances drew in one country after another. On August 4, 1914, after Germany attacked France and Belgium, King George V declared war on behalf of all the British empire. Canada, as part of the empire, was now at war.

"When the call comes, our answer goes at once," declared Sir Wilfrid Laurier. "Ready, aye, ready!" Canada may not have been prepared, but it marched into the war enthusiastically. In Toronto, thousands cheered in support of Britain and sang "God Save the King." In Montreal they sang France's national anthem, "La Marseillaise," as well. Carlstadt, meanwhile, boasted of being the first village in Canada to form a Home Guard to help defend the country.

In small towns and big cities, men rushed to join the army. By September, 30000 Canadian soldiers were marching on the dusty drill fields at Camp Valcartier, near Quebec City. On October 1, the First Contingent of Canada's Expeditionary Force sailed for England, where they endured three cold, dull months of training. Some soldiers worried that the war might end before they could win glory. But it would last longer than the excited young Canadian soldiers could imagine.

A few weeks at the front washed away the Canadians' naive notions about a quick, clean war full of heroism and romance. By April 1915 the Canadians were defending a Belgian town called Ypres, when the Germans attacked with something new in the history of war – poison gas. Gagging and choking, the Canadians managed to hold their positions, but they paid a terrible price. In two savage weeks of fighting over a few hectares of Flanders, 6000 Canadian soldiers died or were wounded. Four Canadians at Ypres won the Victoria Cross, the British empire's highest medal for bravery, and two of them died winning it.

Trench Warfare

Across the rolling plain of Belgium and the north of France, the rival armies lay locked together, unable to advance or retreat, battling over a narrow strip of ground called "no-man's-land." The generals said they must fight on, suffering in their trenches and dying in no-man's-land, until the other side gave in. Instead of marching gloriously into Germany, the Canadians began to dig.

The soldiers lived like moles in a maze of trenches and underground shelters, pounded by shells and bombs. To

H.J. Mowat, Stretcher Bearers. During the First World War, Canada sent "war artists" to capture the experience of Canadians at war. Paintings often did this more poignantly than photographs could.

Damp, dirty, cold, and crowded, the trenches were also dangerous. The soldier looking out of the trench knew he might be in the gunsights of a sniper.

Canadian troops cross "no-man's-land" under fire during the Battle of Vimy Ridge, in April 1917.

advance against the enemy, they had to worm forward among water-filled shell holes and tangles of barbed wire, while snipers and machine-gunners tried to kill them. Between battles, they had to live in the wet, filthy trenches. Their feet, never dry, became infected, and their mud-soaked uniforms teemed with what they called "seam squirrels": itchy, biting lice. Spirits ebbed.

The Newfoundland Regiment discovered the horrors of trench warfare at a place in France called Beaumont-Hamel during the Battle of the Somme, on July 1, 1916. That morning, hundreds of thousands of soldiers of the British empire stormed the enemy lines. The first wave of attackers was slaughtered in no-man's-land. The Newfoundlanders' turn came next. As soon as they left their trenches, the enemy's machine-gunners cut them down in hundreds. In half an hour, the regiment was destroyed, leaving every outpost on the island with someone to mourn. Even after Newfoundland joined Canada in 1949, most Newfoundlanders thought of July first as the anniversary of their tragic losses at Beaumont-Hamel.

At Easter of 1917, the Canadians won a victory. Fighting for the first time as a Canadian corps, they attacked a hill called Vimy Ridge, near Arras, France. They took the ridge in the morning and held it against fierce counterattacks. More than 3000 Canadians died and many more were wounded, but Vimy was a rare victory in the endless trench warfare, and those who survived felt great pride in the Canadian success.

"The Canadians were brought along to head the assault in one great battle after another," wrote the British prime minister. That fall, at Passchendaele, in Belgium, thousands of Canadians died or drowned in the mud while the enemy rained shellfire down on them. The following spring, two field hospitals in France were hit by shellfire, and four Canadian nurses were killed as they tended their patients. There was not much glory in trench warfare.

More than 22 000 Canadians fought a different war – the war in the air. Canada did not yet have its own air

In Flanders Fields

Dr. John McCrae of Guelph, Ontario, sailed off to the First World War as a medical officer with the First Contingent of the Canadian Expeditionary Force, and he went to the front early in 1915. After the terrible battle and poison-gas attack at Ypres that year, he wrote a few lines in memory of a friend who had been killed. The British magazine *Punch* published the poem "In Flanders Fields," and it became the best known of all war poems. But by the end of the war its author was dead. McCrae had died of pneumonia earlier in the year, while still in the army. McCrae's poem expressed what later generations saw as the most important aspect of the First World War: not the glory of victory, but the millions of deaths.

In Flanders fields the poppies blow
Between the crosses, row on row,
    That mark our place; and in the sky
    The larks, still bravely singing, fly
Scarce heard amid the guns below.

We are the Dead. Short days ago
We lived, felt dawn, saw sunset glow,
    Loved, and were loved, and now we lie
        In Flanders fields.

Take up our quarrel with the foe:
To you from failing hands we throw
    The torch; be yours to hold it high.
    If ye break faith with us who die
We shall not sleep, though poppies grow
        In Flanders fields.

Celebrated First World War flying ace Billy Bishop was awarded the Victoria Cross for one of his most daring exploits. Bishop was credited with shooting down seventy-two enemy planes in all.

When Berlin, Ontario, changed its name to Kitchener and heaved a statue of Germany's Kaiser Wilhelm into the lake, not everyone approved. These citizens pulled the Kaiser out again.

force. In 1914, when flyer J.A.D. McCurdy had offered to start an air service, Canada's Minister of Defence had declared, "The aeroplane will never play any part in such a serious business as the defence of a nation, my boy!" But soon Canadian flyers were fighting in biplanes and triplanes that swooped like butterflies high above the horrors of the battlefields below. Eleven of the top twenty-seven "aces" who downed more than thirty aircraft for Britain's Royal Flying Corps hailed from Canada.

Billy Bishop, of Owen Sound, Ontario, had been in continuous trouble at military college before the war, but in aerial combat he found his niche. He was blessed with "the courage of the early morning," always ready to take off at dawn to launch reckless, desperate, close-range attacks on enemy pilots. He emerged from the war with a Victoria Cross and credit for seventy-two victories. His feats inspired other flyers, but few led his charmed life. In 1917, a new pilot could expect to be shot down within about ten days – and there were no parachutes.

Struggles at Home

On the home front in Canada, civilians put their backs into the war effort. They shipped tons of wheat and beef overseas to feed the soldiers. In hurriedly built factories, they churned out bullets and shells, aircraft and ships. People sang patriotic songs, bought war bonds, and donated cigarettes and candy for the troops "over there." Many Canadians became intolerant of anything German, and Canadians of German ancestry felt obliged to show that they were loyal to the British side in the war. In Ontario, the town of Berlin changed its name to Kitchener, after the British war minister, and a statue of the German kaiser was dumped into the lake. "Carlstadt" was a German name, so the people of the Alberta town renamed it Alderson, after the British commander of the Canadians at Ypres.

With so many men off to war, women kept the country going. They gathered in church halls to make

bandages and to knit socks, sweaters, and scarves from endless skeins of khaki-coloured wool. They also took over many jobs once held by men. Before the war was over, 30000 women were working ten-hour days in munitions factories and other war industries. Women were farming, too. In Ontario alone, 2000 female high school and college students, billeted in camps and hostels, helped bring in the harvest each summer.

As soon as the war began, many Canadian women volunteered to work overseas as nurses. More than 3000 white-veiled nursing sisters served as officers in the Canadian forces. They worked in dangerous field hospitals just behind the trenches, or in base hospitals in France and Britain. Because of the colours of the uniforms they wore, the soldiers called them bluebirds.

Since women were doing so much, they wanted a share in making decisions about the country. Women's groups demanded better government, prohibition (the banning of alcohol), and votes for women. Before the war ended, women could vote in federal and most provincial elections. The support women gave to the war effort helped them in their campaign to participate fully in public life. But women were also the backbone of pacifist movements.

During the First World War, posters preached that every conservation effort was important for the war effort.

In wartime there were few men left to help on the farm, and city women were recruited to help bring in the harvests.

Canadian nurses tending wounded soldiers at the Canadian hospital in Paris, in 1917. The patients here are French soldiers.

The sentimental "When Your Boy Comes Back to You" was only one of many songs written and sung during the First World War.

"War is a crime committed by men," wrote feminist Nellie McClung. Laura Hughes campaigned tirelessly against the war, to the fury of her uncle, Sir Sam Hughes, the Minister of Militia.

By 1917, Canadian soldiers were dying in thousands, but fewer young men were now coming forward to join the army. Prime Minister Robert Borden decided that Canada would have to start conscripting men, which meant taking them into the army whether they wanted to join or not. In Alderson, the farmers protested. They were struggling to bring in crops for the war effort, and they could not spare their sons for the army. In Cumberland, British Columbia, a policeman shot fiery labour leader Ginger Goodwin dead when he refused to go into the army. But it was Quebec that exploded in the largest protest over conscription.

Some Quebeckers did join the fighting forces, and distinguished themselves by their bravery. Quebec's 22nd Battalion performed heroic service. Many young soldiers and most of the regiment's officers died in the trenches. One who survived but lost a leg was Georges Vanier, who would one day be Governor General of Canada. Major Talbot Papineau, who was a descendant of the 1837 Rebellion leader Louis-Joseph Papineau, argued that the war could unite French and English in one noble cause.

Papineau's cousin Henri Bourassa disagreed. Bourassa ran Montreal's influential newspaper *Le Devoir*. For years he had written that French and English Canadians should build a new Canadian nationality together. But the way English Canadians went off to fight for Britain convinced him that English Canadians were British first and Canadian second. He felt betrayed. Canada was not in danger, Bourassa told Papineau, and he argued against conscripting unwilling soldiers. Since Ontario was at that time passing new laws to close down French-language schools, Bourassa said that "the Prussians across the Ottawa River" were as dangerous to French Canada as the Prussians who ruled Germany.

Most French Canadians agreed with Bourassa. They did not think this was their war, and they hated the thought of their sons being forced to fight for *les anglais*. Nor were they persuaded by the fact that France was also under attack. Young French Canadians fled to the woods or chopped their fingers off to avoid being dragged into the king's army. But the Conservative Party's plan for conscription was approved by most English-Canadian Liberals. In 1917 a Union government of Conservatives and Liberals, nearly all from English Canada, rammed conscription through Parliament. Some Quebeckers lost faith in Confederation for ever.

The battle over conscription split Wilfrid Laurier's Liberal Party and destroyed his vision of sunny ways and Canadian harmony. "I am branded in Quebec as a traitor to the French," he mourned, "and in Ontario as a traitor to the English. I am neither. I am Canadian." Talbot Papineau, in despair over the hatreds the war had caused, asked to be sent back to the front lines. He was killed at the battle of Passchendaele.

Canada gave all it could to the war effort, including more than 600 000 soldiers from a country of eight million people. Yet Prime Minister Robert Borden discovered that British leaders still treated him as a mere underling, and British commanders threw away Canadian lives without even consulting him. Borden successfully demanded that Canadian leaders sit as equals at the imperial conference table where policy was decided. On the battlefields of France and back home, Canadians were learning to think of themselves as a nation.

Borden feared the war would last into the 1920s, but victory came at last, at 11:00 a.m. on November 11, 1918. In the town of Mons, Belgium, five minutes before 11:00 that morning, a sniper killed an unlucky soldier named George Price, the last Canadian to die in the First World War.

The end of the war brought joy and relief, but the scars left were deep. There were 60 000 dead to mourn, thousands of wounded to care for, and half a million veterans to bring back home. Everyone prayed that these sacrifices had been made in fighting "a war to end wars." Now that it was over, they swore to build a peacetime world worthy of the wartime heroes.

Not many French Canadians were persuaded by recruiting posters like these. Across Canada, but particularly in Quebec, many farmers preferred to keep their sons at home to bring in bumper crops.

The Halifax Explosion

Canada's war effort kept the port of Halifax busier than ever. Early in the morning of December 6, 1917, a Belgian ship named the *Imo* was hurrying through the narrows in front of the town when it collided with a French ship, the *Mont Blanc*. The *Mont Blanc* was loaded with ammunition, and it caught fire.

At six minutes after nine the *Mont Blanc* blew up, and in an instant much of Halifax was destroyed. The blast flattened the city, and fires roared through the ruins. A tidal wave flung broken ships ashore. Sixteen hundred people were killed, and ten thousand – one person in five – lay injured. To make things worse, snow began to fall, and a blizzard raged for days.

For months, the people of Halifax struggled to rebuild their city, while help poured in from the rest of the country and the New England states. Until the atom bomb fell on Hiroshima in 1945, the Halifax explosion was the biggest manmade explosion ever.

The Heartbreaking Twenties

Instead of glory, peace, and prosperity, the postwar years began in hardship and bitterness for many Canadians. In 1918 and 1919, an epidemic of influenza killed 50000, many of them young people. Soldiers coming home found the factories that had boomed in wartime were now out of work and closing their doors. Unemployment went up while wages went down. Even millionaires felt the pinch. Sir Henry Pellatt went broke and had to move out of Casa Loma, his Toronto castle with towers and battlements and secret passages. Prices kept on climbing. Many manufacturers had made fortunes in the war; now workers and soldiers wanted their share of prosperity. To get better wages, they joined unions. In the coal and steel towns of Cape Breton Island, the factories of central Canada, and the west-coast lumber camps, workers organized strikes.

In Winnipeg, workers organized a general strike in May 1919, shutting down the whole city in support of their demands. No factory could open. No trains or buses could run. Even police and firefighters joined the 30000 strikers. Prime Minister Borden sent Mounties and soldiers to fight Canadian workers in the streets. On "Bloody Saturday," police on horseback charged a parade, and one striker was killed. Scores were arrested, and strikers who had been born outside Canada were expelled and sent home. The

Casa Loma was millionaire Sir Henry Pellatt's fantasy castle, built on a bluff overlooking Toronto. After he lost his money, he moved to an apartment.

In 1919, when Winnipeg metal workers struck for better pay and union rights, 30 000 working men and women joined them in a general strike. City leaders called it a conspiracy led by "alien scum." On Bloody Saturday, police on horseback charged crowds of strikers. Strikers retaliated by overturning and burning one of the town's streetcars.

Nobody seemed to be able to beat the world champion "Grads" from Edmonton. They were the best team in women's basketball from 1915 until 1940.

strike was broken, but one of its leaders, a Methodist minister named James S. Woodsworth, began talking about the need for a political party to speak for workers.

There were good times in the 1920s, too, and new inventions that brought excitement and fun. Cars had been rattling around since before the turn of the century, but until after war they were still new and strange. For a while, Prince Edward Island allowed them on the road only three days a week. By the 1920s, quite a few Canadians owned cars. Canadian cars – McLaughlins, Russells, Fossmobiles, and Bourassa Sixes – clanked and clattered down rough Canadian roads. Often they chased horses and buggies off the road, but sometimes a bolting horse would frighten a driver and leave the car upturned in a ditch, its wheels spinning wildly.

In 1919 two British pilots took off from Newfoundland and crossed the Atlantic in a plane, and in that same year several paper companies hired a pilot just back from the war to fly on forest-fire patrols. But for most people aircraft were still mainly for thrills. Pilots "barnstormed" the country in fragile aircraft, flying Tiger Moths or Curtiss Jennies to a farmer's field or large park and charging

Dozens of small machine shops blossomed into carmakers in the early 1900s. Sam McLaughlin's Carriage Works in Oshawa, Ontario, eventually became the giant General Motors plant that is there today.

people for rides or for watching a stunt show.

Canadians continued to develop the wild places of their country. Electric companies dammed the rivers to supply hydro-electric power. Electricity was still new in many Canadian homes, and so were all the wonderful inventions that promised an easier life: vacuum cleaners, electric irons, and radios. The American economy was booming – these years were called "the Roaring Twenties" there – and Americans came north to open pulp mills, mines, and smelters. Prospectors and foresters now roamed the northern "bush" where, in the past, only fur traders and missionaries had visited the Native peoples.

Flying was the best way to get to these regions, and the 1920s became the heyday of the bush pilot. Pilots like "Wop" May came back from the war to fly small planes off lakes and clearings across the North. Flying "by the seat of their pants," they braved snow squalls, half-frozen lakes, and the constant risk of breakdown far from help. In Regina, Roland Groome and Ed Clarke started an air transport service in a field near the Saskatchewan Legislative Building. They carried mail, freight, and even passengers around the country. For a while, Canadian bush planes carried more freight than all the aircraft in the rest of the world combined.

In October 1929, Andy Cruickshank, of Western Canada Airways, joined the search for a party of explorers lost on the Arctic coast. But Cruickshank's ski-equipped Fokker airplane crashed on the ice at Bathurst Inlet. The pilot of another airplane engaged in the search saw the mishap and landed a short distance away. After desperate work in the brief daylight hours, Cruickshank and the other fliers managed to repair the plane and fly out. Soon after, they heard by radio that Inuit hunters had guided the lost explorers to safety.

Tom Thomson, West Wind.
The paintings of Tom Thomson and the Group of Seven gave Canadians a whole new way of looking at the northern land. The paintings became so popular they were hung in schools, banks, and public buildings everywhere.

The adventures of the bush pilots encouraged Canadians to look to the North. So did the work of new young artists. Even before the war, Tom Thomson had begun sketching and painting in the Ontario woods. Whenever he could, he left the city to go canoeing and exploring. The rocks, waters, skies, and blazing autumn leaves inspired Thomson, and he began to paint them. Thomson drowned in Algonquin Park in 1917, and his overturned canoe was found floating nearby. Three years later, Thomson's friends founded the Group of Seven. They no longer wanted to paint in traditional, imitative styles. They developed a bold new way to paint, and their subject was often the lonely northland. Some people hated their dramatic paintings – one critic called them the Hot Mush School – but in a few years the Group of Seven taught Canadians to see the savage beauty of their landscape.

One friend of the Group of Seven, an awkward young doctor and amateur painter named Frederick Banting, would become famous for something quite different. In 1921 he persuaded the University of Toronto to let him spend the summer studying diabetes, a disease that condemned thousands of young people to a slow, wasting death. With luck and skill, Banting and his team discovered the lifesaving insulin treatment. Banting and one of his colleagues won the Nobel Prize for Medicine in 1923.

In 1918 all female citizens over twenty-one had gained the right to vote in federal elections, and one province after another was granting them provincial rights as well. In 1921 Agnes Macphail became the first woman elected to the House of Commons, and in 1929, after a decade-long campaign, women were recognized as "persons" and therefore eligible to be senators and judges. The next year Cairine Wilson became Canada's first woman senator.

The Dirty Thirties

By 1929, stock-market prices were sky high. A stock represents an investment in a business, and it is worth whatever people will pay for it – which means whatever people think the business is worth. In the 1920s many people thought prosperity was just around the corner, and they wanted to put their money into stocks, so prices soared higher and higher. Then, on October 29, 1929, the market "crashed." St. James Street in Montreal was then the financial capital of Canada, and business tycoons and their brokers watched in horror as the value of their investments plunged to almost nothing. Everyone claimed to know some ruined investor who had jumped out of a window in despair. The crash sent the entire Western world into an economic crisis. Nobody wanted to buy Canada's wheat, timber, or minerals any more. The Great Depression settled over the country.

Emily Murphy

Emily Murphy was a writer, reformer, and politician at a time when few Canadian women had even one of those occupations. She was born in Ontario in 1868, and moved to Edmonton, Alberta, in 1903, with her husband, an Anglican minister. Emily Murphy wrote popular books under the pen name "Janey Canuck." She worked for women's causes, and she was appointed police magistrate for Edmonton – the first woman in the British Commonwealth to be named a judge.

On her first day on the magistrate's bench, a defence lawyer challenged her. As a woman, he said, she had no right to sit as a judge, since a woman was not legally a person. Judge Murphy and four other women, including writer Nellie McClung, spent ten years fighting the "Persons Case." In 1928, after the Supreme Court of Canada agreed that women were not legally "persons," the women appealed to England. In 1929 the British Privy Council declared that the ruling was "a relic of days more barbarous than ours," and women were finally recognized as persons.

City people lucky enough still to have jobs saw their wages cut and cut again. One family in three had neither work nor wages. There was no unemployment insurance in those years, and not much welfare. Families who had always had money to give to charity now felt the humiliation of lining up at soup kitchens for a free meal.

Men "on the bum" rode boxcars around the country in search of work. One teenage boy, riding on the roof of a boxcar rolling towards Vancouver, spotted his brother Billy on the roof of another train coming east. Billy had just come from Vancouver, but he jumped across to join his brother anyway. In the Depression years, the destination hardly mattered, since there was little work anywhere. Chasing rumours of jobs here and there, the "hoboes" fought with railway police, slept in "hobo jungles" near the railyards, and begged meals at back doors and farm gates. When they found a home that gave a meal and a little kindness, they left a mark on the fencepost to let other drifters know.

In Newfoundland fishing ports, people could at least catch some food, but Newfoundland needed to sell fish too, and few countries could afford to buy. Newfoundland, not yet part of Canada, had been a self-governing dominion, but in 1934 its government went bankrupt. The British government had to take over and manage it from London, making it a colony once again. The three Maritime provinces suffered almost as much. Once Atlantic Canada had been the richest, brightest, most go-ahead part of the country, but since Confederation it had been slipping behind. Maritimers streamed to the United States in search of work. Many were hungry and out of work in Quebec and Ontario, too. Factories closed their doors, and families were forced to live on the charity of their communities. But the Depression was not as hard on central Canada as it was on the West.

The 1930s were terrible times to be a prairie farmer. Parts of the Prairies that usually got all the rain they needed became a "dust bowl." Month after month, hot, dry winds beat against the homesteads. The topsoil turned to dust and black blizzards carried it away. Even where the crops survived, prices were so low that wheat was hardly worth harvesting. The "Golden West" of Wilfrid Laurier's day

Children from remote areas of northern Ontario in the "school train," a passenger car-turned-classroom. This photo was taken in Chapleau.

A dust storm approaches Pearce, Alberta. In the Dirty Thirties, drought did as much damage to the farms of the Prairie Provinces as the low crop prices of the Great Depression.

seemed to be drifting away like dust on the wind.

Calgary lawyer Richard Bedford Bennett became Prime Minister of Canada in 1930, soon after the Depression struck. In 1932 he established work camps run by the army, where 20 000 single men worked for twenty cents a day on backbreaking construction projects. The men hated the camps, and thousands went on strike. They and many other people who were suffering in the hard times set out by train for Ottawa to protest. Bennett did not want thousands of angry men confronting him on the steps of Parliament, and he told the police to stop the "On to Ottawa" marchers in Regina. On July 1, 1935, the police and the marchers clashed in the Regina market square, and two men were killed in the fighting.

The Dionne quintuplets from Callander, Ontario, became the world's sweethearts during the Great Depression.

What was to be done about the bad times? Every political leader had a different prescription. In 1932, J.S. Woodsworth, who had been arrested after Winnipeg's Bloody Saturday in 1919, founded the Co-operative Commonwealth Federation. The CCF wanted the government to take over the economy in the name of the people, to help people in need, and to provide work for the unemployed. In Alberta, Premier William ("Bible Bill") Aberhart preached Social Credit: let the government print money and give it to the people to spend. In Ottawa, Prime Minister Bennett promised his "New Deal" would save the day by reorganizing the economy and providing unemployment insurance. Hungry prairie families were not impressed. They hitched their scrawny horses to the cars they had bought in better times and used them as wagons. (They called these vehicles "Bennett Buggies" to let the prime minister know whom they blamed for their troubles.) In the fall of 1935, Canadians voted Bennett out of office.

He was replaced by a Liberal government headed by William Lyon Mackenzie King, who had been prime minister during most of the 1920s. (King was the grandson of William Lyon Mackenzie, a leader of the Rebellion of 1837.)

In earlier years, Canada had been less than hospitable to immigrants whose skin colour, dress, or language marked them as "different." That tendency grew stronger

The unemployed workers who formed the "On-to-Ottawa" movement to confront the politicians had no money for transportation. They simply climbed aboard boxcars. There was no trouble at Medicine Hat; but in Regina, police were gathering to prevent them from going farther.

Home from school, a boy drops his books in front of the family radio. In the 1930s, radios were larger than televisions are today.

Trick cyclists entertain at Toronto's Canadian National Exhibition in the 1930s.

in Depression days, when people were struggling to survive and competing for scarce jobs. Since 1885, Chinese immigrants had been forced to pay a humiliating fee called a "head tax" to enter Canada. In 1934, the government made a change: it decided that no Chinese at all could enter Canada. And walls were going up against other minorities. At a time when the Nazis in Germany were persecuting Jews, Canada was turning away Jewish immigrants.

In the midst of Depression hardships, Canadian Native people – even war veterans who had risked their lives for the country – were told to "live off the land" and were denied government help. At the same time, Native children were still being taken from their families and put in boarding schools where they lost touch with their traditions and were forbidden to speak their own languages. Leaders like Andrew Paull, a Squamish from British Columbia, and F.O. Loft, a war veteran from the Six Nations Reserve in southern Ontario, began organizing their people to demand respect for themselves and the rights guaranteed to them in the treaties they had signed.

Escaping from the Bad Times

In those hard times, people did not want to think about their troubles. They escaped into "dime" novels, dance parties, movies – mostly American-made movies – and radio. Gathered around their radios, families listened to many American programs, but the most popular programs came from the Canadian Broadcasting Corporation, which was created in 1936. Any family with enough money for a radio could listen to Canadian news, dance to Don Messer's country dance band, or follow football and hockey, play by play. East and West had been competing in football for the Grey Cup since 1921, but the East (which set the rules) won every year until 1935, when the Winnipeg Blue Bombers won the championship for the West.

"Hockey Night in Canada" was becoming a Saturday night tradition. Fans across the country jumped up in excitement when broadcaster Foster Hewitt screamed his catch-phrase, "He shoots! He scores!" One night in 1937, Canada's greatest hockey star of the decade, Howie Morenz, broke his leg during a game in Montreal. The injury became infected and, in those days before antibiotics, Morenz died of blood poisoning. The Montreal Canadiens held his funeral at centre-ice at the Montreal Forum, while hockey fans everywhere mourned.

War Again

In the spring of 1939, King George VI and Queen Elizabeth came to visit Canada. It was the first time a reigning monarch had toured Canada, and it was a bright moment in a dark time. In Ottawa, the king and queen dedicated the national memorial to the dead of the First World War. They travelled across the country by train, stopping in

Doctor Bethune

In 1936, a small band of Canadians called the Mackenzie-Papineau Battalion went off to fight a dictatorship in the civil war that was then raging in Spain. Dr. Norman Bethune, from Gravenhurst, Ontario, also went to Spain to help in the war. Bethune invented a blood-transfusion system that, for the first time, could deliver blood to wounded men right on the battlefield. Although the Mac-Paps were on the losing side in the Spanish Civil War, Bethune's blood transfusions saved many lives.

Bethune went off to another war, this time in China, where he worked for the rebel Communist army of Mao Zedong. He not only assisted the sick and wounded, he also taught and invented new medical procedures. But in the fall of 1939, operating without surgical gloves because medical supplies were scarce, he got blood poisoning and died.

Mao Zedong wrote an essay, "In Memory of Norman Bethune," in which he told his followers that they should all have Bethune's devotion to other people. When Mao's Communist party took power in China, he made sure that the Canadian doctor was known all over the country as a great hero. Canada has been known in China from that day as the home of Dr. Norman Bethune.

Norman Bethune
in Canada / au Canada
诺尔曼·白求恩在加拿大

39

CANADA

In 1940, Warren Bernard, age five, says goodbye to his father, Private Jack Bernard, as the British Columbia Regiment marches through New Westminster, B.C., on its way to the war.

In 1940, when Britain's cities were being bombed, thousands of British children were evacuated to Canada to spend the war years in safety with Canadian families. After the war was over, some returned here to live.

all the cities along the way. In smaller towns, the train slowed while the royal couple waved to people from the rear platform.

Only a few months later, Canada went to war again. Dictatorial regimes which glorified war and conquest ruled Germany, Italy, and Japan, and in the late 1930s they began attacking their weaker neighbours. On September 1, 1939, Adolf Hitler's German army invaded Poland, and Britain declared war on Germany. This time Canada decided for itself whether to go to war. Most Canadians agreed that the dictators had to be stopped, but there was not much cheering. Remembering the terrible times of 1914–1918, Canada went grimly into the war on September 10, 1939. This time, no one thought it would all be over in a few weeks.

After crushing Poland, Germany occupied Denmark, Norway, Luxembourg, The Netherlands, and Belgium. In June 1940 France also surrendered, leaving Britain without European allies. Canada was Britain's chief ally against the dictators for more than a year. But in 1941 Germany invaded the Soviet Union, which then joined the fight against Hitler. The Soviet Union's Joseph Stalin was a ruthless dictator, but because he was fighting the Nazis "Uncle Joe" became a hero in Canadian eyes. At the end of 1941, when Japanese bombers attacked the American naval base at Pearl Harbor in Hawaii, the United States joined the Allies and the war became a global struggle.

"My King and Queen"

by Alixe Hambleton, who remembers the visit.

I was nine years old when King George and Queen Elizabeth came to Regina. It was May 25, 1939, a lovely, warm spring day. Children from all the neighbouring towns and villages, like my town of Lumsden, were taken to the exhibition grounds to see them. Dressed in our best, complete with medals hung on red, white, and blue ribbons, we lined up around the racetrack. We all had flags to wave.

At last the king and queen arrived. They were driven slowly around the track in an open car. The king wore a suit. The queen wore a blue coat over a dress, and a hat with plumes. We cheered and waved our flags. They smiled and waved at us.

Afterwards, I had lunch with my parents in a restaurant. "They didn't look anything like a king and queen." I sighed. "They looked ordinary."

After lunch, Mother and I went shopping. Dad had business to do, so we met at another restaurant for dinner. Two restaurants and ice cream for dessert after dinner all in one day – a rare treat in 1939!

"We have one more stop to make," my father said. "Wait and see," was the only answer I got when I asked about it. We went to the railway station and my father said something to one of the railway officials. The man smiled at me and led us outside to the train yard and over the tracks to where the royal train was standing.

We didn't have to wait long. Suddenly all the lights in the station yard went on. Then the king and queen appeared on the observation platform of the last car of their train, not a dozen metres from where we stood. The king was in full dress suit with all his medals on his chest. And the queen had on a beautiful long white brocade gown with the blue sash of the Order of the Garter across it. On her head she had a diamond tiara. They really looked like a king and queen. Not at all ordinary. They waved, then the train was off down the track.

My father had spent the afternoon finding out when the royal train was leaving and whether the royal couple would be on the observation platform after their formal reception at the Saskatchewan Hotel. I've never forgotten my father's gift of my king and queen.

During the Second World War, Canadians went all over the world to fight by land, sea, and air. In 1941, Canadian soldiers sailed away to defend the British colony of Hong Kong. After the Japanese army overran the colony, more than 500 Canadians died horribly, in battle or in the prison camps. Most Canadian soldiers, however, went to Britain. The army trained there, waiting for a chance to liberate Europe. Farley Mowat, a young soldier in the Canadian Army's First Division, wrote: "The troops fought imaginary battles in the English fields and lanes until they grew numb with fatigue." The soldiers complained about the cold and the damp and the food, and many swore that after the war they would never eat Brussels sprouts again.

On August 19, 1942, 5000 Canadian soldiers crossed the English Channel to attack a little town on the French coast called Dieppe. The Allied generals had hoped to seize the town for a day, but when the Canadians landed

The battle of Dieppe is shown in vivid detail in Charles Comfort's painting Dieppe Raid.

on the stony beaches under the cliffs of Dieppe, the Germans were waiting in fortified bunkers that bristled with guns. It was a disaster for the Allies, and a tragedy for Canada. Barely 2000 Canadian soldiers got safely back to England that night.

In July 1943, the First Canadian Division – with General Guy Simonds in command – invaded Sicily alongside British and American soldiers. In September 1943 Italy surrendered, but the many German troops in Italy fought on. Soon the Canadians were grateful for what they had learned while training in those "imaginary battles" in England. They marched and fought from the scorching heat of Sicily to the mud and rain and snow of northern Italy. The Moro River, Regalbuto, Rimini, and Ortona became Canadian battlefields as memorable as Vimy and Passchendaele in the First World War.

During the grim battle for the Italian town of Ortona, where more than 2000 Canadians were killed or wounded, Captain Paul Triquet and his company fought for seven hours to capture the farm of Casa Berardi at the town's gateway. Only Triquet and 14 of his 81 men were still alive when they captured it – and then the Germans counter-attacked. "*Ils ne passeront pas!* [They shall not pass!]" became Triquet's rallying cry, as he and his men held out for nine more hours – losing 5 more men – before Canadian reinforcements arrived. Triquet was awarded the Victoria Cross.

This Second World War recruiting poster hoped to convince prospective soldiers that joining the war effort was the noble thing to do.

At Sea and in the Air

All through the war, Canadian warships rolled and pitched through the North Atlantic, guarding the convoys of ships that were Britain's lifeline of supplies and troops. The first convoy sailed out of Halifax in September 1939, escorted by two Canadian destroyers. That convoy crossed the Atlantic safely, but soon German submarines called U-boats (from the German *Unterseeboote*) were sinking hundreds of Allied ships. Some nights the naval escorts chased

Paul Goranson, Dorsal Gunner. Thousands of Canadians flew as gunners, navigators, pilots, bombardiers, and radio operators on night missions over German territory. This gunner is aboard a two-engined Wellington bomber.

desperately after submarines they could not see, as tankers and freighters exploded and burned around them. In one terrible three-day running battle off Greenland in 1943, HMCS *St. Croix* was struck by a torpedo and sank. Her captain and most of the crew went down with her. Another ship plucked a few survivors from the water, but it too was torpedoed, and only three sailors survived – including one who had come from the *St. Croix*.

Sometimes the navy had to fight within sight of home, when German U-boats sailed into the Gulf and up the St. Lawrence River to torpedo ships and to land spies. One U-boat even sank the passenger ferry *Caribou* on its route between Nova Scotia and Newfoundland, killing 137 passengers and crew.

Many Canadian sailors served in small ships called corvettes, and fought the rough seas of the North Atlantic as hard as they fought the German submarines. "Corvettes roll in a heavy dew," sailors said. Wet, cold, frightened, and crowded, they sailed from Halifax, Sydney, or "Newfiejohn" (St. John's) to get the convoys through to Britain. Canada had started the war with a very small navy, but by the end of the war it had the fourth-largest navy in the world.

Secret Agents

Sergeant-Major Lucien Dumais of Montreal landed on the beach at Dieppe with the Fusiliers Mont-Royal on August 19, 1942. More than a hundred of the Fusiliers died there that day, and Dumais was captured. But on the way to a prisoner-of-war camp in Germany, Dumais jumped from the train and escaped. Although France was occupied by German troops, French civilians helped him make his way to the coast, and he got safely back to England.

Dumais's war was far from over, for he volunteered to go back to France as a secret agent. In November 1943, a small plane dropped him and another Canadian, Raymond Labrosse, in northern France. Soon they had created an escape network for Allied flyers who were shot down in France.

Dumais, Labrosse, and their French comrades made false papers for the flyers. Some they led into Spain. Many of them they guided to the coast, then radioed for small boats that slipped across the Channel from England to pick up the escapees. If they were caught they would be shot. In all, 307 flyers escaped along the network, and Dumais and Labrosse never lost a man.

In 1940, Canadians were among the handful of fighter pilots in sleek Hurricanes and Spitfires who defended Britain against waves of German air attacks. More flyers later served in four-engined bombers that targeted German cities and factories. Thirty bombing missions were a "tour of duty," but long before their tours were done, many young Canadians were blown out of the sky. Some managed to parachute behind enemy lines, and French, Dutch, or Belgian families hid them and helped them to safety. One of the 10000 who died was Andrew Mynarski of Winnipeg. He was about to parachute to safety when he saw one of his fellow crewmen trapped in their burning plane. Mynarski fought unsuccessfully to free him, and he jumped only when his own clothes were aflame. Mynarski died of his burns, but the trapped gunner rode the bomber to the ground and lived.

Another Canadian contribution to the air war took place on this side of the Atlantic. Because the country had the wide-open spaces that novice flyers needed – and because it was far away from hostile action – Canada became, in the words of the American president, Franklin Roosevelt, "the aerodrome of democracy." At places like Debert, Summerside, and Chatham in the Maritimes, St-Hubert and Hagersville in central Canada, and Gimli, Weyburn, High River, and Patricia Bay in the West, Canadians and other British Commonwealth airmen learned to be pilots, navigators, gunners, and bombardiers. The training was fast. Those who passed got their wings and went overseas to war.

Prime Minister William Lyon Mackenzie King – and Pat.

On the Home Front

Canada's wartime prime minister was William Lyon Mackenzie King, a fussy bachelor. Although no one knew it at the time, King used a crystal ball to ask his dead mother for advice. Fortunately, he ignored her "ideas" when he disagreed with them.

In the first years of the war, all of Canada's soldiers

were volunteers. King did not want the country – and his Liberal Party – to be divided over conscription as it had been in the First World War. "Parliament will decide," he liked to say when he wanted to avoid making some decision. If Canadians were drafted, he declared, they would serve at home, not in the fighting overseas. "Zombies," the fighting soldiers called these conscripts contemptuously. Later King added, "Not necessarily conscription, but conscription if necessary." Finally, in 1944, the army was desperate for fighting men, and Parliament changed the rules. Sixteen thousand "Zombies" were sent to fight in Europe. But although there was bitterness on both sides of the conscription debate, King's delaying tactics may have kept the country from suffering a conscription crisis even more divisive than the one during the previous war.

Many German and Italian prisoners of war were shipped to camps in Canada. Only one German prisoner, Lieutenant Franz von Werra, ever escaped from Canada. He jumped from a train near Prescott, Ontario, and crossed the border, then fled through the United States to Mexico. "The one that got away" got all the way back to Germany, only to be killed in action later in the war.

Red Cross nursing sisters, 1940.

Hanorie Umiarjuaq

She was a tough little ship with a tough skipper. The *St. Roch* was a floating RCMP station that patrolled the far northern islands of Arctic Canada. Her skipper was Sergeant Henry Larsen, a Norwegian Canadian who must have had the blood of Norse adventurers in his veins. The Inuit called him "Hanoric Umiarjuaq," meaning "Henry with the big ship." Skipper Larsen and the *St. Roch* cruised the northern waters for twenty-two years, from 1928 to 1950.

In 1940, during the Second World War, Skipper Larsen got the exciting orders he wanted. He was to leave Vancouver and sail for Halifax, through the Northwest Passage. The Norwegian explorer Roald Amundsen had sailed the passage from east to west, but no one had ever gone west to east.

Two years later, after three summers of sailing and two dark winters locked in Arctic ice, the *St. Roch* lay trapped in the ice floes of Bellot Strait. The strait is thirty kilometres long and barely one kilometre wide, with sheer cliffs towering on either side. Larsen was beginning to fear they would have to pass another long winter in the ice.

Then the tide began to drive the ice floes and the *St. Roch* forward. Faster and faster they raced along. The pressure of ice on the hull was immense, and the ship groaned and twisted, but the timbers held and soon the *St. Roch* shot out into clear water. In six weeks she was in Halifax.

In 1944 Larsen and the *St. Roch* set out again, and went east to west through the Northwest Passage in just eighty-six days, the first ship to do the voyage both ways. In 1950 the *St. Roch* sailed south and became the first ship to go right around North America. Today the stalwart little *St. Roch* is on display at the Maritime Museum in Vancouver.

Women as well as men went into uniform. They persuaded the air force and the army to form women's corps, and finally the navy did too. Forty-five thousand women joined the forces during the war. "My parents were rather upset – they felt the army was no place for a girl!" recalled one woman who enlisted in 1942 at the age of twenty. Generals and admirals often felt the same. The services never paid women what men received, and they tried to keep them in "women's jobs" as typists or cooks.

A postman delivering ration books to the Brocketts of London, Ontario, in 1942. During the war many foods, clothing, gasoline, and tires were rationed.

Paraskeva Clark was one of dozens of Canadian artists who painted Canada at war. Maintenance Jobs in the Hangar *shows women working on the Harvard trainers that would be used to train pilots for service overseas, and in Canada, too.*

Yet one father who had been wounded at Vimy Ridge in 1917 said it was the "proudest moment of his life" when his daughter enlisted in the forces. Women did become pilots, codebreakers, and mechanics, and 7000 women served in Europe. Seventy-one were killed by German bombing.

Many more women – 800000 of them – remained civilians and went into offices and factories during the war. Some of them studied to become mechanics, welders, and electricians, but most working women learned a trade on the job, where they got less pay and less chance of promotion than men did. Nevertheless, so many women went to work in factories during the war that, for the first time, industries started daycare centres to look after their children. For the first time, women drove city buses and taxis, and took over many other jobs that had always been called men's work.

The Canadian economy was going full tilt, producing food, weapons, and equipment for the war. There was a great effort not to waste anything, and every hand was needed. Even children pitched in, collecting paper and

scrap metal. Old fur coats were made into warm vests for Canadian sailors, and anyone buying toothpaste had to turn in the old tube for recycling. Even old bones were collected, to make glue and explosives.

After Japan entered the war and bombed Pearl Harbor, British Columbians were terrified of a Japanese invasion. They vented their fear and rage on the 22 000 Japanese Canadians, accusing them of being spies and enemy agents. Most Japanese Canadians lived along British Columbia's Pacific coast. In 1942, these families were rounded up and sent to camps far inland – even though many of these people were Canadian citizens, and many had never even been to Japan. Then the government seized and sold off their houses, cars, fishing boats, and all their property. British Columbia's Japanese-Canadian community was destroyed. Hardly anyone protested. "There's a war on," people said, to excuse this ruthless action. The Japanese Canadians did not receive reparations and an apology from the Canadian government for the injury done to them until 1989.

At Slocan, B.C., Japanese Canadians forcibly removed from the British Columbia coast in 1942 struggle off an open truck with the few belongings left to them.

June 6, 1944

D day, 7:00 a.m., at Juno Beach, Normandy. As a torpedo boat roars past, a landing craft crowded with soldiers of the Royal Winnipeg Rifles rumbles toward the coast of France. The machine guns of the enemy await them.

All night, bombers had pounded the enemy fortifications on the shore. As dawn broke, ships like HMCS *Algonquin* of the Canadian navy began to fire shells at hundreds of targets. But only the infantry could finish the job. Thousands of soldiers had to leave their transport ships and head ashore in smaller landing craft.

The landing craft carrying the soldiers rolled and lurched in two-metre waves. The enemy began firing furiously when the Royal Winnipegs were still 700 metres from Juno Beach. Some landing craft blew up and sank, some were trapped by hidden obstacles beneath the surf. But at 7:49 a.m. the Royal Winnipegs hit the beach and raced through the enemy gunfire. The soldiers entered the French town of Courseulles, then pushed on inland.

The soldiers of the Royal Winnipeg Rifles, along with the rest of the Canadian, British, and American regiments, paid a terrible price that morning of June 6, 1944 – but the Allies had begun the liberation of Europe.

The End of the War

In wartime comics, Canadian superheroes like Dixon of the Mounted and Nelvana of the Northern Lights battled Nazis and saboteurs in every issue of Active *and* Triumph *comics.*

At dawn on June 6, 1944 – D day – the Allied forces launched a massive invasion of German-occupied France. As part of an immense operation that used 7000 ships and 11 000 aircraft, the Canadians fought their way ashore on "Juno Beach," one of the five D-day landing beaches in Normandy, France. The Western Allies advanced slowly towards Germany, while the army of the Soviet Union pushed in on the Germans from the east. Early in 1945, the Canadians liberated most of The Netherlands from German occupation. They reached Amsterdam at the end of the "hunger winter," during which thousands of people had died of illness, cold, and starvation. With the Canadians came food and medical supplies. The country welcomed them with wild celebrations.

Caught between the Western Allies on one side and the Russians on the other, Germany was finally defeated. Adolf Hitler killed himself and Germany surrendered in May 1945. But the war with Japan was still going on. Twenty thousand Canadian soldiers were ordered to the Pacific, and sixty ships of the Canadian navy headed there as well. Then the United States dropped a secret weapon the Allies had been working on all through the war: the atomic bomb. The first bomb fell on the Japanese city of Hiroshima on August 6, 1945. In an instant, the city vanished beneath a rolling, boiling mushroom cloud. For the first time, a nuclear weapon had destroyed a city and its people in a single deadly flash of radiation and fire. Three days later, a second bomb destroyed the seaport of Nagasaki. Japan surrendered at once, and the Second World War was over.

In the spring of 1945, as they fought their way across Europe, driving the Germans out, Canadian soldiers confronted horrors worse than those they had shared on the battlefield. When they liberated the concentration camps, they found them crowded with heaped bodies and starving survivors – and grisly relics of victims gassed and cremated. Hitler's Nazis had planned to create a "master race," and they had set out to murder all the Jews of Europe, and many other groups as well. At least six million people had died in the concentration camps, and Canadians began to realize that some of those people had been turned back from Canadian shores in the years before the war. Now, at last, thousands of death-camp survivors were admitted to Canada as refugees. So were other Europeans, whose homes and families had been shattered by the fighting.

As the war ended, the Soviet Union and its Western allies quickly became rivals. British war leader Winston Churchill said that an "Iron Curtain" had fallen across Europe, dividing the wartime allies into Communists in the East and non-Communists in the West. The "Cold War" was about to begin. But Canadians were rejoicing over the end of the Second World War. And after three stormy decades, they were also about to enter a time of prosperity and hope at home.

Thousands of Canadian soldiers who went overseas married British and Dutch women. In 1946 nearly 50 000 women and 22 000 children, like these aboard ship, followed the soldiers to new lives in Canada.

Chapter 2

The Flying Years

Down by the Fraser River in Richmond, B.C., kids dropped their bikes and crowded along the fence at the end of the Sea Island Airport runway. It was June 1, 1948, and the North Star was coming in.

The North Star was Trans-Canada Airlines' brand-new passenger plane, and it was making its first Montreal-to-Vancouver flight. TCA had made the very first passenger flight across Canada just nine years earlier. That trip had taken more than a day, and passengers had had to wear oxygen masks while the Lockheed Electra struggled over the Rockies. Now the North Star's four powerful engines cut the flight to thirteen hours, and the airplane carried forty passengers high above the clouds in a pressurized cabin. It was the biggest, fastest, most luxurious passenger aircraft Canadians had seen – and it had been built in Canada.

In the years after the Second World War, Canada was flying high. Air travel made it possible to leap across continents and oceans. At Chalk River, Ontario, scientists were making electricity, using a nuclear reactor. In Saskatoon, Professor Harold Johns developed the cobalt radiation "bomb" that targeted cancerous tumours. The fearsome scientific discoveries that had won the war seemed to promise a better future in peacetime.

When the war ended in 1945, more than a million men and women came out of the armed forces. Half of the men, and about 7000 women, had been overseas, and almost 50000 of them had married "war brides" (or "grooms", in a few cases) while they were there. In May 1946, four trains of ten cars each left Montreal, filled with brides going to new families and husbands whom many barely knew.

Many war brides found it hard to adjust to their new homes and to Canadians, who seemed so different. A few took "the thousand-dollar cure" – a trip back home that convinced them Canada offered more than war-ravaged Europe.

When Farley Mowat came home from the war, he was happy to turn in his infantry badges for a set of textbooks

Previous pages:
Ottawa's Parliament Hill has been the site of many demonstration marches and protest gatherings, as Canadians exercise their right to dissent.

and a jam-packed classroom at the University of Toronto. Canada was helping "vets" (war veterans) pay for homes or for schooling. Mowat was one of thousands who were eager to get an education and become doctors, lawyers, and business people – or even, like Mowat, writers. Despite their years of war, many of them were barely out of their teens.

Canadians came out of the Second World War proud of what they had done as a nation. They also remembered the hard times after the previous war, and the agonizing Depression of the thirties, when each region of the country had seemed to suffer on its own. Now more prosperous times had come.

The DC-4 North Star, built by Canadair at Montreal, was the workhorse of the trans-Canadian air routes in the late 1940s and early 1950s.

Proud Growing Regions

In British Columbia, returning veterans found plenty of work cutting timber, refining minerals into precious resources, or catching and canning salmon. By the early 1950s, B.C. had a brash new premier, W.A.C. Bennett, who loved to brag about the way his province was growing. His rivals called him "Wacky," but, wacky or not, Bennett governed the province for twenty years. British Columbians built roads through the mountains, launched ferries to ply the coastal waters, and dammed their wild rivers for electric power. Bennett loved to flash his beaming smile and talk of "Beautiful British Columbia." He told British Columbians that their province was a paradise, and that they were envied by people who had to live anywhere else.

Farley Mowat Meets a Wolf

After the Second World War, Farley Mowat became a naturalist and a writer. The Canadian government sent him to the barrenlands of northern Manitoba to study wolves. Wolves, he was told, were fierce, pitiless killers, and unless they were destroyed they would slaughter the caribou herds. So, even when he heard what seemed to be a young cub crying for its lost mother, Mowat approached cautiously:

As I neared the crest of the ridge I got down on my stomach (practicing the fieldcraft I had learned in the Boy Scouts) and cautiously inched my way the last few feet.

My head came slowly over the crest – and there was my quarry. He was lying down, evidently resting after his mournful singsong, and his nose was about six feet from mine. We stared at one another in silence. I do not know what went on in his massive skull, but my head was full of the most disturbing thoughts. I was peering straight into the amber gaze of a fully grown arctic wolf, who probably weighed more than I did, and who was certainly a lot better versed in close-combat techniques than I would ever be.

For some seconds neither of us moved but continued to stare hypnotically into one another's eyes. The wolf was the first to break the spell. With a spring which would have done justice to a Russian dancer, he leaped about a yard straight into the air and came down running. The textbooks say a wolf can run twenty-five miles an hour, but this one did not appear to be running, so much as flying low. Within seconds he had vanished from my sight.

My own reaction was not so dramatic, although I may very well have set some sort of a record for a cross-country traverse myself. My return over the river was accomplished with such verve that I paddled the canoe almost her full length up on the beach on the other side. Then, remembering my responsibilities to my scientific supplies, I entered the cabin, barred the door, and regardless of the discomfort caused by the stench of the debris on the floor made myself as comfortable as I could on top of the table for the balance of the short-lived night.

It had been a strenuous interlude, but I could congratulate myself that I had, at last, established contact – no matter how briefly – with the study species.

In his fine and funny book *Never Cry Wolf*, Mowat tells how he gradually learned to appreciate the wolf. It was hunters, not wolves, who were killing off the caribou – and the wolf as well.

Throughout his life, Farley Mowat has celebrated the land and the animals of Canada, and those people who live in harmony with them. Long before the "environment" became a popular cause, his books exposed the cruel and destructive ways our society treats nature.

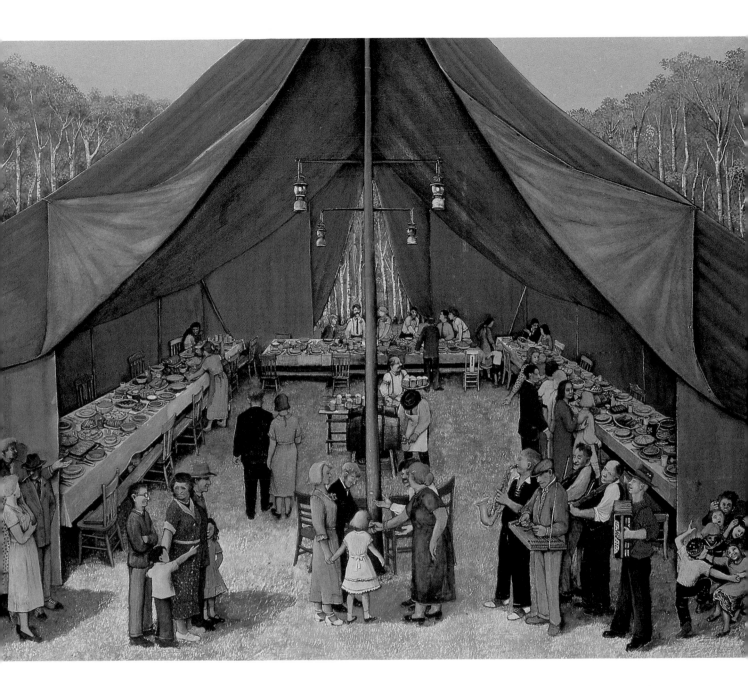

After the war, the Prairie Provinces were finally able to shake off the twenty terrible years of the Dustbowl and the Depression. In Alberta, an oil well "blowout" at Leduc announced the start of a new era. Oil prospectors had drilled 133 dry holes around Leduc before they struck oil in February 1947. They renamed that hole Leduc Number One, and soon 1200 more productive wells "came in" to join it. Alberta discovered that the oil business had the rowdy excitement of the old cowboy days – and there was

William Kurelek, Manitoba Party. *Kurelek painted a magical series of pictures re-creating the simple joys of a prairie boy's childhood.*

Nineteen-year-old champion Barbara Ann Scott, from Ottawa, was the country's most popular celebrity after she won the Olympic gold medal in figure skating in 1948.

Tommy Douglas, one of the first socialists to win political power in Canada, was premier of Saskatchewan and then national leader of the New Democratic Party.

more money in it. Oilmen from Texas came up to Calgary to drill for oil and gas and to build pipelines to transport them. Alberta became the home of a try-anything, free-wheeling style of doing things, in business and in government.

The farmers of Saskatchewan, after all the hard years of struggling together against duststorms and low prices, preferred co-operation to competing for wealth in Alberta's risk-taking style. Saskatchewan had pioneered in creating co-operative businesses, owned by the farmers who used them, to ship grain and bring in supplies. In 1944 it elected Canada's first socialist government, led by a wise-cracking, passionate Baptist minister named Tommy Douglas. Douglas's government introduced new social services, including Canada's first medicare plan, run by the government and available to all. Later, Douglas was elected national leader of the New Democratic Party, which became Canada's third-largest political party.

In Ontario and Quebec, factory gates opened wide to the returning veterans. In the small town of Oakville, Ontario, the Ford Motor Company opened a huge automobile plant, and for a while Oakville was the richest town in Canada. In Hamilton, Ontario, steel mills rolled out the steel for Alberta's oil pipelines. Quebec also had new factories. General Motors built an auto plant in Ste-Thérèse, and gleaming North Star aircraft rolled out of a plant in Montreal. For nearly a century Ontario had had many factories making goods for the whole country, but such industries were newer in Quebec, and they brought many changes.

In the 1940s and 1950s, Premier Maurice Duplessis ruled Quebec. Duplessis assured French-speaking Quebeckers that the Catholic Church and the family farm would preserve their French-Canadian way of life in the midst of English-speaking North America. His iron hand came down hard on anyone who wanted to change things. His ideal Quebec was a place where people lived on farms, obeyed their priests, and raised big families. But not all Quebeckers were like that. Many were leaving the farms to work in big cities or mining towns. Instead of living the way their ancestors had always done, Quebeckers were starting to live much the way people did all over North America. Duplessis made Quebec look changeless during those years, but changes were brewing underneath.

The biggest change in Atlantic Canada came in Newfoundland and Labrador. Newfoundland's government had collapsed, bankrupt, in 1935, and the colony was again being run by Britain. During the war, the island had been vital to Allied air and naval forces. But what would Newfoundland do now the war was over? "Join Canada!" urged Joseph Smallwood, an unsuccessful pig-farmer who had become a popular radio host. "Joey" burned with the conviction that Newfoundlanders had to join the modern world. The way to do it, he declared, was to become Canada's tenth province. Newfoundlanders were not so certain – old cries about the "Canadian wolf" were raised again. Some wanted Newfoundland to remain proudly alone, while others wanted to join the United States. After fierce debates that kept nearly everyone on the island glued to the radio, Newfoundlanders agreed to have a referendum, or general vote, on whether they would join Canada.

Smallwood and the Confederation forces barely won the referendum, and Newfoundland and Labrador became Canada's tenth province in 1949. Smallwood, a new "Father of Confederation," became Premier of Newfoundland. He would hold the office for more than twenty years. As part of his plan to bring Newfoundland into the modern world, he urged his people to burn their fishing boats and to work in mills and factories instead. Like many people in the 1950s, he believed that prosperity was just around the corner.

At midnight on March 31, 1949, Louis St. Laurent welcomed Newfoundland into Confederation. St. Laurent, who was nicknamed "Uncle Louis" (though he was rather cold and stiff in public), had become prime minister when Mackenzie King retired in 1948, and he led Canada into the prosperous 1950s. Now that the country could afford it, Ottawa moved ahead with unemployment insurance,

After a narrow win in a stormy campaign to settle Newfoundland's future, Joseph Smallwood signed the document making Newfoundland the tenth province of Canada in 1949.

old-age pensions, and "baby bonus" payments. If hard times like the 1930s ever came again, there would be a "safety net" of government programs to protect people against suffering.

Canada in the Wide World

Canadian diplomat Lester Pearson won the Nobel Peace Prize for his work in creating the first United Nations peacekeeping force. Pearson went on to be Prime Minister of Canada.

In the 1950s, Canada liked to call itself a "middle power": not the biggest, but not the smallest, either. It had played an important part in the war, and it expected to continue in the same way in peacetime. Canada helped Europe recover from the damage done by the war, and shared in the founding of a new world organization, the United Nations, to help the world's nations work together more effectively. In 1950, Canada helped to create the Colombo Plan, in which the wealthier countries of the British Commonwealth promised to help the poorer ones to develop their economies. This was the start of Canada's foreign aid program.

In 1956, when war erupted over control of the Suez Canal in Egypt, Canadian diplomat Lester Pearson led the way in creating the first United Nations peacekeeping force, and another Canadian, General E.L.M. Burns, led the peacekeepers who stood between the warring sides. Pearson won the Nobel Peace Prize for his work on the Suez crisis, and in 1958 he succeeded Louis St. Laurent as leader of the Liberal Party.

Canadian soldiers would serve on many more United Nations peace missions, but peacekeeping could not make the world a safe place. Soon after the war, Canada became part of a deep, fierce rivalry that divided East from West. The Soviet Union, or U.S.S.R., born in the Russian Revolution of 1917, had become a great power during its battle against Nazi Germany. When the war ended, its armies imposed Communist dictatorships on the nations of Eastern Europe. Germany itself was split into two parts, with the eastern part under Soviet control. The U.S.S.R. promised these states prosperity, and it preached Communist revolution to the rest of the world.

In 1945, Igor Gouzenko, a clerk at the Soviet Union's embassy in Ottawa, fled from the embassy with his wife and children. He carried proof that Soviet spies were at work in Canada and the United States, prying into military secrets and trying to learn details about the atom bomb. At first, no one in Ottawa would believe him, and the Soviets nearly recaptured him. But when the public in Canada and around the world heard his story, fear of Communist spies and secret agents began to grow. By 1949, when Mao Zedong led a peasant army to victory over the corrupt government of China and made China a Communist state, many in the West (Canada, Western Europe, the United States, and their allies) feared that Communism might take over the world the way Hitler and the Nazis had tried to do. Just four years after defeating the Nazi conquest, the Western world began arming itself against Communism.

In 1949, Canada and eleven other Western nations founded NATO, the North Atlantic Treaty Organization, for their mutual self-defence, and Canadian troops went back to Europe once again. All along the borders dividing Eastern Europe from the West, the armies of the Soviet Union and the NATO allies faced each other. Year after year, as politicians blustered and manoeuvred, the world watched to see if fighting would erupt. This tense, dangerous stand-off was called "the Cold War."

In 1950, war between Communists and anti-Communists broke out in the Asian nation of Korea. Canada sent ships and soldiers as part of the U.N. forces. In April 1951, a handful of soldiers from a regiment called the Princess Patricia's Canadian Light Infantry became the first Canadian ground troops to fight in Korea. Chinese troops were driving the United Nations forces southward when the Princess Pat's dug in on Hill 677 to defend the southern capital, Seoul. The South Korean soldiers had been beaten farther north, and as they came streaming back in retreat, the Canadians confronted a Chinese army.

The Princess Pat's spent the night of April 24–25 outnumbered and surrounded, but they held Hill 677 in

No one knew what Igor Gouzenko looked like. After he exposed Soviet spying in 1945 and 1946, he wore a disguise to protect himself from revenge. In 1954 he wrote a novel about the Soviet Union.

Under a camouflage net, a Canadian soldier gets some sleep on the engine of his tank beside the Imjin River in Korea. Canadian soldiers have earned an unmatched record for their services to United Nations peace-keeping forces all over the world.

terrifying hand-to-hand fights against waves of attackers. In the morning the enemy advance slowed and stopped. Reinforcements from Canada's allies came up, and the lines around Seoul held. But it had been a near thing. In the end, the Korean War wound down into a kind of truce in 1953. The Canadians came home, except for the five hundred who died there.

Canadian forces also went into the Arctic. During the Cold War, Canadians and Americans feared that Soviet bombers might suddenly swoop over the North Pole to attack their countries. To defend North America, they built the twenty-two radar stations of the DEW (Distant Early Warning) Line, more than 8000 kilometres long. There were terrible new weapons in the world. Both the United States and the U.S.S.R. had atomic bombs like those that had obliterated Hiroshima in 1945, and soon scientists made even more powerful hydrogen bombs. Long-range bombers could drop them anywhere, and if either side started a war, the other would immediately retaliate. Aircraft, missiles, and submarines stood on alert night and day, waiting for the dreadful orders that could level whole cities. People everywhere began to realize that nuclear war could destroy the world. That fear – the "balance of terror" – kept both sides from launching a nuclear attack, all through the Cold War.

Home in the Suburbs

Boom! In the 1950s, the population exploded. At least, it seemed that way. Hard times and war had kept Canadians from having big families in the 1930s and 1940s. But in the "baby boom" years, streets, schools, and playgrounds were crowded with more kids than anyone could remember. The millions of children born between the Second World War and 1960 became adults between the late 1960s and the 1980s, and they made a bulge in the population.

Four million Canadian babies were born in the 1950s, and many families needed new homes. Few homes had

been built in the 1930s, when no one had money to build or buy them, and during the war materials and workmen had been scarce. In the 1950s, Canada went on a building spree, producing more than a million new houses in ten years. In a few years, the shape of Canadian cities changed completely.

Don Mills, eight hundred hectares of farmland a few miles up the Don River from Toronto, was built as a new kind of community, the model Canadian "suburb." In Don Mills, the working bustle of the city seemed far away. Everyone lived in bungalows with big "picture windows" that looked out over wide lawns to curving streets where children played street hockey. Soon suburbs were sprouting around every city in the country – Fraserview and Surrey near Vancouver, Wildwood near Winnipeg, Cowie Hill and Sackville outside Halifax.

For people who had to live downtown or couldn't afford a house, there was another new kind of home, the "high-rise." Tall apartment towers sprouted like forests in downtown Vancouver and Toronto, housing far more people than the old low-rise buildings – but also making city crowding and traffic jams worse. Old neighbourhoods close to downtown were bulldozed for "public housing" apartment buildings. New and modern seemed better than old and traditional in the 1950s, and many useful, wellbuilt buildings – a record in brick and stone of the country's history – were demolished just because they needed repairs or were out of fashion.

Instead of shopping downtown on Main Street, suburban Canadians headed for another invention of the 1950s: the shopping centre. Park Royal, in West Vancouver, claimed to be Canada's first shopping centre, but soon every suburb had one. At first a shopping centre meant a row of stores facing a parking lot, but soon the centres turned indoors and became malls.

As the cities spread out into suburbs, more people needed cars. Canadians bought three million cars in the fifties. A big, bright new Ford or a Chevrolet with swooping fins and plenty of chrome was often the first car a family

One of Canada's first pop stars, Paul Anka was sixteen when he first had a big hit, with "Diana," a song about his babysitter in Ottawa.

In every playground, the hula hoop was the hottest trend of the late 1950s. It was not an easy task to keep four hula hoops spinning at once, but this girl seems to be a real champion.

Cars of the American "Big Three" automakers, many of which were made at Windsor, Oakville, or Oshawa, Ontario, ruled the roads in the 1950s. Fins, chrome, and gadgets were the fashion.

had ever owned. Gasoline was cheap, and the whole country seemed to be on wheels. Canadians drove to work, to the shopping centre, the drive-in movie, the hamburger stand, and to the cottage or camp. For the first time, many Canadians – not just wealthy ones – took vacations away from home.

The country's first superhighway, the Queen Elizabeth Way from Toronto to the U.S border, had opened just before the war. In the fifties and sixties, the exit ramps, interchanges, and overpasses of superhighways blossomed around every big city. The federal government and the provinces got together to build the Trans-Canada Highway from St. John's to Victoria. Trains still hauled freight and grain across the country, but the day of the railway was passing, and soon passenger trains would be running half empty. If Canadians couldn't travel by air, they wanted to go by highway.

Canadians became "consumers." They had money to spend on cars and appliances and all kinds of gadgets and hobbies. Most of them had grown up with electric light and power, but now they could afford to fill their new homes with freezers, convenience foods, washer-dryers, and "hi-fi" record players. Most of the new fads and luxuries came from the United States, the biggest, richest, most powerful country in the world. In the fifties, things labelled "Made in Japan" were still laughed at as junk.

The hottest new appliance was the television set. Canadians who lived near the border hooked their small sets up to wobbly antennas and tried to pick up a black-and-white picture from an American station just across the border. CBC Television went on the air in 1952, and gradually every city saw its own stations begin broadcasting. It was great being able to see the Toronto Maple Leafs and Montreal Canadiens play, instead of trying to follow hockey action on the radio. If your family was the first on the block to have a set, you invited the neighbours in to watch.

The 1950s also invented rock and roll – and teenagers. Too often, before then, children had had few chances to be children. Many had worked hard to help support their families, and many never finished school. By the 1950s and 1960s, however, teenagers lived a life much different from what their grandparents had known. Instead of following in their parents' footsteps and learning grownup tasks and responsibilities, postwar teenagers were busy with their own interests and activities. They had their own slang and their own fashions. They were still going to school, and they might go to college later. If they worked, it was to add to their allowance, and they spent their money as they liked. They could buy a new record by Paul Anka, a kid from Ottawa who became a pop star in the United States, or save up for one of the new little transistor radios so that they could carry their music everywhere. Boys dreamed of buying an old car and turning it into a "souped-up" hot rod. Girls wore their cardigans buttoned up the back, soaked their crinolines in sugar-water to make them stiff, and swooned over American movie stars like Marlon Brando and James Dean.

During the 1950s, Canadians began to take more

Sixteen-year-old Marilyn Bell fought oil slicks and lamprey eels, as well as fatigue, to become, on September 9, 1954, the first person to swim across Lake Ontario. It took her twenty-one hours, and radio and newspapers followed every stroke she took.

interest in being Canadian, as the links with Britain weakened. Canada now ran its own international affairs, and the country was becoming more of a player in the world – partly because of its peacekeeping and other United Nations activities. In 1952, Vincent Massey became the first Canadian-born governor general (at least since Pierre Rigaud de Vaudreuil, the last governor general of New France).

New Canadians

In the 1950s, new Canadians mostly still came down the gangplanks of transatlantic passenger ships in Halifax or Montreal. Many groups had enriched Canada with their hard work on farms and in towns across the nation, but three-quarters of all Canadians had British or French roots, and most immigrants still came from Europe.

By the middle of the twentieth century, Canada's population had reached fourteen million. Some were the children, grandchildren, and great-grandchildren of immigrants who had poured into Canada in the years before the First World War. Jewish communities were now strong in Montreal, Winnipeg, and some other cities. Finnish culture thrived in northern Ontario. Ukrainian was widely spoken on the Prairies, and Vancouver had one of the largest Chinese communities outside China. But except for Chinese and South Asians on the west coast, American Blacks in Ontario and Nova Scotia, and a few other groups, Canada had not accepted many immigrants from non-white or non-European backgrounds.

After the Second World War, Canada reopened its doors to immigrants. Nearly three million arrived in just twenty years. Instead of just coming by ship, they came by plane, to airports all across Canada. And the proportion of British and northern European immigrants became lower. Southern Europeans were the first groups to grow more numerous; Italian communities expanded rapidly in the cities during the 1950s, and Greek and Portuguese communities soon appeared. Non-European immigrants also began to arrive. They came from the islands of the Caribbean, from India and Pakistan, from Korea and Hong Kong, and from many other countries. People of hundreds of languages and backgrounds now enriched Canada with their traditions.

The newcomers brought their customs and beliefs with them. Sikh and Buddhist temples stood beside Jewish synagogues or Catholic or Baptist churches, and whole sections of cities sprouted street signs in Chinese, Portuguese, or Italian. Suddenly, there were shops selling food, clothing, music, books, and artworks that were new, startling, and fascinating to many Canadians. The 1950s and 1960s opened Canada to the tastes and styles of the world. It was becoming a multicultural nation.

Many of the immigrants came to Canada for the same reason as the early colonists: they hoped that hard work in a new land would provide a better life for their children. But in the troubled postwar world, Canada also became a haven for refugees from oppression and war. Often the refugees arrived poor and penniless, but many were skilled and ambitious people who quickly made their mark in their new country. In 1956, when the tanks of the Soviet Union crushed an uprising in Hungary, 30000 Hungarian exiles came to Canada. In 1968, when Soviet tanks rolled into Czechoslovakia, more refugees fled to Canada. During the 1960s, when the United States was fighting a war in Vietnam, 32000 young Americans immigrated here, rather than be drafted and forced to take part in the conflict. Some of the refugees dreamed of returning to their homelands one day, but most hoped to make new lives in Canada.

In 1957, Canadians voted out Louis St. Laurent and the Liberal Party, which had ruled Canada since 1935, and elected a prime minister who passionately believed that people of every background could share "One Canada." John Diefenbaker's parents had come to Saskatchewan as homesteaders in 1904. "When we got rich," he liked to say, "we moved to a sod hut." He never forgot his humble roots. He spoke out for "ordinary" Canadians, and he

A colourful parade marks the celebration of Chinese New Year in Vancouver.

Crises in other parts of the world have often brought new communities to Canada. These Hungarians fled after the failure of their rebellion against Soviet rule in 1956.

John Diefenbaker campaigning in 1957. Canadians across the country rallied to the fiery speeches of the man from Prince Albert, Saskatchewan. They gave his Conservative Party the biggest win in Canadian history.

wanted all Canadians to share the opportunities the country offered. In 1958, "Dief the Chief" won the biggest election victory in Canadian history. His Conservative Party took 208 of the 265 seats in the House of Commons.

Diefenbaker had a "vision of the North." Instead of huddling along the border, watching American television, he said, Canadians should go north, to lay down roads, open mines and mills, and create new towns. Workers started uranium mines in Uranium City, Saskatchewan, and Elliot Lake, Ontario. They built a new city around the iron ore mines of Schefferville, Quebec, which shipped eight million tonnes a year down the railway to the new port of Sept-Iles. In Kitimat, British Columbia, a brand-new city grew up around a new aluminum smelter. The North seemed like a treasure trove of riches waiting to be discovered. Still, most Canadians stayed in the south.

Diefenbaker's vision of the North never made much room for the Native nations there, though his government did allow Native people to vote in Canadian elections for the first time. In the 1950s, the number of Native people in Canada began to increase, after centuries of slow decline. Soon Native leaders would be finding new ways to defend their people and to reclaim their lands and rights.

"Il faut que ça change!"

Quebec's powerful premier, Maurice Duplessis, died suddenly in the late summer of 1959. Duplessis had been Quebec's uncrowned king, and few could imagine life without *le Chef*, the boss. He had always told his people that they must cling to their traditional ways or their unique culture would be swamped by English-speaking North America. But after his death, Quebec began to stir.

In the 1960s, Quebec decided to take on the world, not shelter from it. But its people were as determined as ever not to be swallowed up by the English-speaking population around them. French Quebeckers declared that they were ready and able to run their own affairs. They were not going to be pushed around by the government in Ottawa, or by the wealthy English-speaking minority which had run most of the big businesses in Quebec. "*Maîtres chez nous,*" cried the new Quebec premier, Jean Lesage – "Masters in our own house."

Quebeckers saw that they would need skilled, educated people, and they began opening new schools and universities around the province. A huge power dam, Manic-5, which provided power for the growing cities and industries, became a symbol of the energy surging through Quebec. "*Il faut que ça change!*" was a popular saying in the new Quebec. "Things have to change!"

René Lévesque, a fiery broadcaster with a cigarette always at the corner of his mouth, was Premier Lesage's most controversial, colourful minister. Lévesque demanded that the federal government give more power to Quebec. He spoke passionately of Quebec's rights and the wrongs done to French Canadians, and he became a hero to a new generation of people who chose to be called "Québécois," not "French Canadians."

"What does Quebec want?" asked English Canadians. Before long, Lévesque proposed an answer – sovereignty! He believed the future for Quebec was as an independent country, running its own affairs without interference from the rest of Canada.

English Canada was alarmed by this talk of "separatism." The government in Ottawa promised to renew Confederation, to make French Canadians feel they were truly equal to English Canadians throughout the country. It began to promote "bilingualism and bicul-turalism" as the future for all of Canada. That annoyed many English Canadians, who complained that French was being "shoved down their throats." However, these measures were not enough to satisfy René Lévesque. He walked out of Premier Lesage's government and founded a new political movement which became the Parti Québécois. The Parti Québécois promised to take Quebec out of Confederation. It wanted Quebec to gain all the powers of an independent country, and then

Rarely seen without a cigarette, René Lévesque fought for Quebec's independence with a passion that made him one of the most loved – and most feared – politicians in Canada.

Mannumi Shagu's Woman and Children, *an Inuit sculpture from Cape Dorset, Baffin Island.*

negotiate a new kind of relationship with Canada.

There was another organization, the Front de Libération du Québec, which wanted more than an independent country. This secret group wanted a complete change in Quebec – a revolution – and it was ready to use violence to get it. In 1963, FLQ bombs began exploding in mailboxes and office buildings around Montreal. People across Canada wondered whether the turmoil in Quebec would produce a new version of Confederation, an independent Quebec, or bloodshed in the streets.

In the 1960s, not only Quebec but the whole country seemed eager for change. In Canada and many other parts of the world, the older "baby boomers" had reached their teenage years. Because those were prosperous times, they had more spending money than previous generations of youth. Their favourite musicians became international celebrities, like the Beatles from England, who swept to the top of Canadian music charts late in 1963. Their fashions, like miniskirts, blue jeans, and long hair, even began to spread to adults who wanted to appear youthful or "with

When "hippie" and "straight" lifestyles clashed in communities like Toronto's Yorkville and Vancouver's Gastown, conflict with the police often followed.

it" (as they said in the 1960s). Late in the decade, some of the young people became "hippies," rejecting the technology and ambition of the time and preaching international peace and love. They grew their hair long and wore beads and earrings from Eastern countries like India and Afghanistan. Some dropped out of school. Some gave up meat and alcohol, and turned to herbal tea and marijuana. Some rejected the idea of marriage, and lived in groups in rundown urban neighbourhoods like Yorkville in Toronto and Gastown in Vancouver. Others went "back to the land," where they tried living in communes and raising organic foods.

Many sixties youth had high ideals. In 1961, university students founded Canadian Universities Service Overseas, or CUSO, which sent young Canadians abroad to help poor people in underdeveloped countries. Later, many university campuses became stormy places as students marched in protests, trying to change how the universities and all of society worked. They also wanted to change the way Canada and the United States got along. They argued that Canada was too closely tied to the United States. Canada was becoming an American colony, cried the new Canadian nationalists. They wanted a country independent of foreign control, making its own plans.

It wasn't only young people who were unhappy with old ways. Canadian women were changing their lives, too. More and more women were taking paid jobs and working outside the home. By 1967, there were as many women in the work force as there had been during the Second World War. However, newspapers still ran separate ads for "Help wanted, male" and "Help wanted, female," and most of the powerful, well-paid positions still seemed to be reserved for men. Ellen Fairclough, a chartered accountant, became the first woman Cabinet minister in 1957. Lawyer and writer Judy LaMarsh was a prominent politician in the sixties. However, they were exceptions. Women still faced discrimination when they aspired to "men's" jobs – and met with opposition when they talked about changing the way men ran the world.

Montreal college students march in protest along Rue Ste-Catherine in October 1968. Students everywhere marched, for various causes, in the 1960s.

In the late fifties, when nine-year-old Abigail Hoffman wanted to play on a minor-league hockey team, she had to pretend to be a boy named "Ab" Hoffman. By the 1960s Abby Hoffman was a star athlete competing for Canada in the Olympics, but girls still could not play organized hockey. Things were starting to change, however – in sports, at work, everywhere. By 1967, the women's movement had pushed the government into studying the status of women in Canada. There would be great changes in the next few decades.

Canada's Birthday Party

The year 1967 was Canada's one-hundredth birthday, and the nation threw itself an exuberant birthday party. Canadians surprised themselves with a sense of pride and a sense of fun.

Across the land, towns and communities started work on imaginative centennial projects. One Manitoba town put in a sewer system and made a July-first bonfire of its outhouses. An Alberta town produced a flying-saucer landing pad. Charlottetown, the "Cradle of Confederation," had led the way with its Confederation Centre, and hundreds of other towns opened centennial community centres, centennial libraries, or centennial arenas. The new maple leaf flag blossomed everywhere. It had been chosen as the national flag just two years earlier, after fierce debates about its design and colour, and now young Canadians travelling in Europe or India, or hitchhiking down the Trans-Canada Highway, carried the red and white emblem sewn on their backpacks.

The world's fair in Montreal, Expo 67, became the highlight of Centennial Year. A few months before the fair opened, the islands in the St. Lawrence where it would be held were a muddy, chaotic construction site, and many nervous Canadians predicted disaster. Instead, Expo blossomed into perhaps the most exciting world's fair ever. Its pavilions displayed the best of all nations, and its theme

How Canada Got Its Flag

After Confederation in 1867, Canada remained part of the British empire, and the flag it flew was either Britain's Union Jack or the Red Ensign with the Canadian coat of arms. As the country slowly shed its colonial past, Canadians started to consider what a truly Canadian flag should look like.

In 1964, Parliament began to debate the design of a national flag, and hundreds of designs were presented. The Union Jack, the fleur-de-lis, and the beaver all had their supporters. Gradually the maple leaf won out. But would it be one maple leaf or three? For months, legislators wrangled, editorials thundered, letter-writers argued, and protesters shouted over the look of the flag.

At first Parliament proposed three red maple leaves on a white back-ground with blue bars on each side. But red soon replaced the blue, and a citizens' group named "The Committee for a Single Maple Leaf" fought for a simple, clear image at the centre of the flag. At last the government closed off the debate. On February 15, 1965, Canada's new flag was officially unfurled – the bold, distinctive red maple leaf (see following page) that is now recognized around the world.

YUKON

• Whitehorse

Great Bear Lake

NORTHWEST TERRITORIES

Yellowknife

Great Slave Lake

BRITISH COLUMBIA

ALBERTA

Edmonton

MANITOBA

Victoria

SASKATCHEWAN

Regina

Lake Winnipeg

Winnipeg

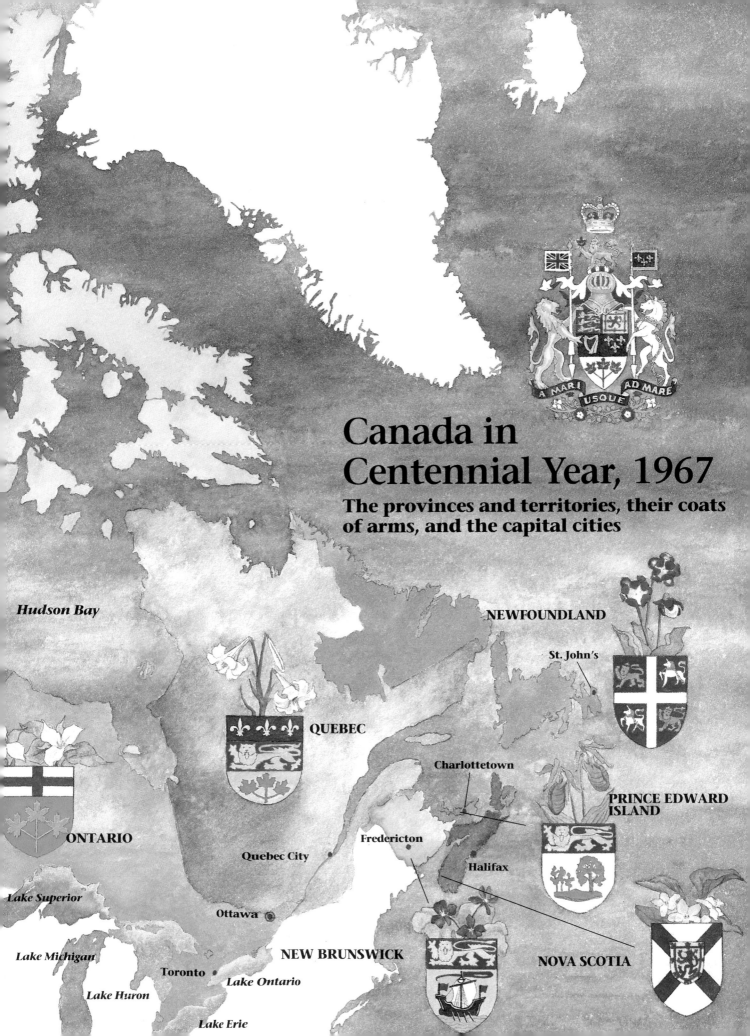

Canada in Centennial Year, 1967

The provinces and territories, their coats of arms, and the capital cities

Hudson Bay

NEWFOUNDLAND

St. John's

QUEBEC

Charlottetown

PRINCE EDWARD ISLAND

ONTARIO

Fredericton

Quebec City

Halifax

Lake Superior

Ottawa

Lake Michigan

NEW BRUNSWICK

NOVA SCOTIA

Toronto   Lake Ontario

Lake Huron

Lake Erie

"Terre des Hommes/Man and His World," expressed a new mood that was bubbling up in Canada. Canada welcomed the world to Expo 67, and fifty million visitors came – two visitors for every Canadian.

By 1967, the North Star that had been so exciting in 1948 had long since gone to the scrap heap. Canada had joined the jet age in 1960, when Trans-Canada Airlines' DC-8 cut the Toronto-Vancouver flying time to five hours. Under its new name, Air Canada, the national airline would soon be making the same trip with jumbo jets carrying 350 passengers. Astronauts were travelling into space, and just two years after the centennial, men would walk on the moon. No one knew just where Canada was going – but suddenly the ride looked exciting.

Coming Together – Flying Apart

Now that Canadians could fly across the country in the time it took to eat a meal and watch a movie, it seemed that Canada should be more united than ever before. Instead, it seemed to be flying apart. Everything was being questioned. New groups challenged the status quo. The pride people felt in their own regions collided with the struggle to build a unified nation. More and more Canadians were asking hard questions about the way the country was put together.

Canada had a new prime minister. John Diefenbaker's Conservative Party had been replaced by Lester Pearson's Liberals in 1963, and when Pearson retired in 1968, Pierre Elliott Trudeau took over. With him came "Trudeaumania." Trudeau was younger than most Canadian prime ministers had been. Perfectly bilingual, he was clever in both French and English. On the campaign trail, he could debate with students, draw admiring crowds at the shopping centre, and show off on the diving board back at his hotel. He had the same excitement as Expo 67, and he won the federal election of 1968. For a while, Canada's new prime minister was as popular as a rock star.

Expo 67 in Montreal was successful – and a lot of fun. Centennial year was like that.

Underneath the glamour, Pierre Trudeau could be tough. His obsession was Confederation and Quebec's place in it. He rejected the idea of independence for Quebec. Instead, he wanted a Canada in which French Canadians were full and equal partners, and he was willing to fight for that. In October 1970, when the FLQ kidnapped a politician, Pierre Laporte, and a British diplomat, many young Québécois cheered. Some of the province's leaders talked of making a deal with the terrorists. Trudeau sent in the army instead.

The ordinary freedoms that Canadians take for granted were suspended. In Montreal, police arrested hundreds of "suspects" in the middle of the night. Soldiers patrolled the streets, and helicopters roared overhead. The "October Crisis" shook all of Canada. Here and there, civil-libertarians spoke out against the government's assault on civil rights, but as the crisis raged, Quebec and its people looked revolution in the face and turned away. The terrorists murdered Pierre Laporte, but there was no more support for violence and terror in Quebec. After the kidnappers were allowed to escape to Cuba in exchange for freeing their British hostage, the FLQ simply vanished. Quebec would decide its future democratically.

Prime Minister Trudeau set about making the French language equal to English in the government of Canada. He brought French-speaking Canadians to Ottawa, and he made English-Canadian civil servants learn French. French signs joined English ones in federal buildings and projects across the country. Many English Canadians responded positively, by sending their children to French-immersion schools so they could take their place in a bilingual Canada. Many others complained that "the French" were taking over the government and the country.

During the 1970s, Pierre Trudeau's government borrowed and spent money lavishly. Canadians wanted new and better programs for the elderly, the handicapped, minorities, women, children, and the poor. Companies demanded government support for risky or expensive projects. "Crown corporations" (companies owned by

Pierre Elliott Trudeau was a man with a style of his own, here with a rose in his lapel and "Trudeau-mania" surrounding him.

the government) invested in oil exploration, railways, and many other industries. All this was costly, but the government believed that using the taxes paid by citizens to achieve the country's ambitions was a good thing.

Battle of the Titans

While Pierre Trudeau was determined to build a united, bilingual Canada, René Lévesque held to his own vision of an independent Quebec – with a passion equal to Trudeau's. When Lévesque's Parti Québécois swept to power in Quebec in 1976, Trudeau and Lévesque confronted each other in a battle for the future of Quebec and Confederation.

The Parti Québécois had promised to consult the people of Quebec before breaking up Canada. On May 15, 1980, the people of the province voted in a referendum that asked them to say *"Oui"* or *"Non"* to a plan that would make Quebec "sovereign" (that is, independent) yet still associated with the rest of Canada in some way that would be decided later. Lévesque led the forces for the *"Oui"* and "sovereignty-association," and Trudeau led the forces for

The Greatest Goal

Canadians always knew Canadian hockey players were the best in the world. In 1972 the Soviet Union challenged Canada to prove it, in an eight-game series pitting their best players against the best Canadian professionals of the National Hockey League.

Most Canadians thought the only question was how many goals their team would win by. But by the time Team Canada headed for the Soviet Union, after four games at home, the country was in shock. The Soviet

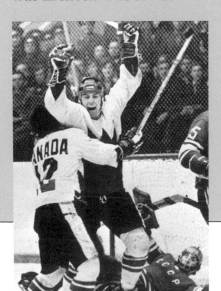

team had lost only one game! The score was two to one, with one tie.

Canada lost the first game in Moscow, too, but then Paul Henderson of the Toronto Maple Leafs scored the winning goal in games six and seven. He became a national hero with his final goal, the most famous goal in hockey history, which won game eight – and the series – with just thirty-four seconds left to play.

On the lawns of Parliament on April 17, 1982, Prime Minister Pierre Trudeau watches as Queen Elizabeth signs the agreement that brought Canada's constitution, the British North America Act, to Canada.

the *"Non"* and for renewed Confederation. Canada held its breath as Quebec voted. The result was 60-40 for the *"Non."* Separatism had been rejected.

Trudeau had promised that, if Quebec voted for Canada, the nation's constitution, the British North America Act, would be changed. The BNA Act still sat in Britain, and ever since it had been written in 1867 there had been no way for Canadians to amend it except by acting through the British Parliament. In 1981, Trudeau led the effort to set rules by which Canada would change the BNA Act itself, and despite René Lévesque's protests, he succeeded. In April 1982, the constitution finally came to Canada. In a rain-soaked ceremony on Parliament Hill, Canadians took over the power to change their own constitution, and added a Charter of Rights and Freedoms to protect individual liberties. In Quebec the Parti Québécois held on to power for a few more years, but it seemed that separatism was dead.

Energy and Ecology

While Trudeau and Lévesque fought their battle, Canada and the world had been changing fast.

In 1973, during a crisis in the Middle East, the Arab countries – which produced most of the world's oil – stopped selling oil to Japan, Europe, and North America. Since gasoline is made from oil, there were soon long lineups at service stations. Governments brought in new laws to conserve oil, and fuel prices shot upwards. Oil soon began to flow from the Middle East again, but something

No ordinary mall – you can ride a balloon, a roller-coaster, or a submarine at the West Edmonton Mall.

had changed. Oil, the lifeblood of the modern world, suddenly seemed scarce and very precious.

Alberta, which had most of Canada's oil and natural gas, enjoyed a "boom." In Calgary, new bank towers and oil company buildings displayed Alberta's wealth. From all over western Canada, shoppers flocked to the West Edmonton Mall, the largest shopping centre in the world – which soon had its own indoor roller coaster, a pool with submarines and sharks, an ice rink, and a hotel. Alberta also took pride in its new medical research industries, its theatres, and its museums, including the Tyrrell Museum of Paleontology near Drumheller.

As money and people flowed to western Canada, Albertans declared that westerners would no longer simply provide cheap resources for central Canada. Western Canada wanted a bigger share in Confederation. Some nervous easterners murmured about "western separatism," but western leaders declared that "the West wants in." Alberta led the way in demanding new powers for the provinces, and changes in Ottawa to make all the provinces full partners in Canada.

In 1979, Edmonton's hockey team, the Oilers, joined the National Hockey League. Until 1967 Montreal and Toronto had had the only Canadian teams in the league, but by the end of the 1970s there were teams from Quebec City to Vancouver. Edmonton's team, led by an eighteen-year-old sensation named Wayne Gretzky, was soon the best of all. No one had ever scored or set up goals the way "the Great Gretzky" did.

The world was still desperate for oil, and oil companies soon turned their explorations to the stormy Grand Banks of Newfoundland. The search paid off when floating oil platforms struck oil on the Hibernia field, 200 kilometres out from St. John's. After half a century of hard times, Maritimers hoped their region would begin to prosper from the oil that would flow from Hibernia. They were eager to support themselves and, like Alberta, Atlantic Canada "wanted in." Newfoundland led the fight for local control of oil and fisheries.

When Number 99, "the Great One," played for the Edmonton Oilers, it was the hottest team in hockey. Gretzky turned professional at age seventeen, the youngest major-league athlete in North America.

There was oil beneath the seas and islands of the Arctic, too. The Americans had never officially recognized Canada's claim to the northern waters, and in 1969 they challenged both Canada and the forbidding Arctic when they sent a huge oil tanker, the *Manhattan*, through the Northwest Passage without asking Canadian permission. In the end, however, the *Manhattan* needed help from the Canadian icebreaker *John A. Macdonald* to avoid being trapped in the ice.

One way Canada could get oil from the Arctic Sea was by carrying it, in what would be the world's longest pipeline, across the Yukon and south through the Mackenzie Valley. In 1974 Judge Thomas Berger was appointed to investigate the pipeline plan. Judge Berger talked to the people most affected, the Dene people of the Mackenzie Valley. They

Nuclear Energy

When the Second World War ended with the dropping of two atomic bombs, Canadian scientists began to study how to use atomic power peacefully to generate electricity. The result was the CANDU (Canadian Deuterium Uranium) reactor. CANDU reactors use Canada's abundant supplies of natural uranium, protected by immersion in deuterium, or "heavy water."

Today CANDU reactors in Ontario, Quebec, and New Brunswick provide about 12 per cent of Canada's electricity. But they also create concern. Many people fear that a nuclear accident, like the one that happened at Chernobyl in the Soviet Union in 1986, could endanger many lives and pollute the atmosphere for centuries. And since used nuclear fuel remains radio-active for thousands of years, safe places to store it have to be found.

Each CANDU reactor is a brilliant example of Canadian science and engineering, and CANDU scientists are confident that no Chernobyl-type accident is possible. But the risks of nuclear power show us the dangers of technology. As we worry more about pollution, and as our supplies of oil run out, the problem of creating cheap, safe electrical power will continue to face Canadians.

told him that they still hunted and trapped in their valley homeland, and that a pipeline might destroy their fragile valley. "Deep in the glass and concrete of your world, you are stealing my soul, my spirit," said Dene chief Frank T'Seleie. Judge Berger recommended that the Mackenzie pipeline be postponed, and the government agreed. Despite southern Canada's thirst for oil, the concerns of Native people were beginning to be heard.

As the hunt for resources went on, Canadians began to think more about "ecology." In the fall of 1971, a rundown, crazily painted old ship named *Phyllis Cormack* sailed out of Vancouver for the remote Alaskan island of Amchitka. The United States intended to test a nuclear bomb on Amchitka. The small band of British Columbian protesters aboard the ship wanted to stop them and warn the world about the dangers of nuclear radiation.

The voyage of the *Phyllis Cormack* did not stop the bomb from being exploded, but it gave the world a new word and a new organization: Greenpeace. In hundreds of colourful ways, Greenpeace told the world's people about the damage being done to our planet and the need to protect it. To save the whales from being hunted to extinction, Greenpeace's ships confronted the whaling fleets on the high seas. To preserve the forests, its members blocked logging roads in British Columbia's rainforest. Canadians were beginning to see that progress brought comfort and leisure, but also polluted the air and water. Four billion people crowded the planet in the early 1970s, and there would be six billion by the year 2000. Canada's population was small, but each Canadian used up far more of the world's resources than a person in one of the poorer, developing countries.

Greenpeace began in British Columbia but it defended the environment in protest actions around the world. British Columbia was like that; after a hundred years as

Whenever they send their fragile Zodiacs to confront whaling ships or naval ships with nuclear weapons, Greenpeace's campaigners always get lots of attention.

Whooping Cranes

Each spring, the whooping cranes fly north from the Gulf of Mexico to their nesting grounds in the bulrush marshes of northern Alberta. Whooping cranes are pure white, except for small red and black markings on their heads and their two-metre wings, and they are the tallest birds in North America. Their migration makes a spectacular sight for any nature lover.

But fifty years ago only fifteen whooping cranes, the last wild whooping cranes in the world, made that flight. Another irreplaceable species stood at the edge of extinction as the cranes' distinctive whoop fell silent.

Since then, Canadian and American wildlife experts have fought to save the whooping cranes from hunters, droughts, and the draining of the marshlands they need. Slowly the whooping cranes have recovered.

Today they number more than 150, and wildlife experts are beginning to believe the species will survive. If so, they will be one of the first species ever rescued by careful conservation efforts. For the whooping crane and many other endangered species, the fight goes on.

Canadian writing for children blossomed in the 1970s and 1980s through the work of authors such as Dennis Lee and Margaret Laurence.

part of Canada, the province still looked out to the Pacific Ocean and the rest of the world. In the 1970s and 1980s, Vancouver grew and prospered as Canada's gateway to the rapidly growing nations of the Pacific. British Columbians were also fiercely proud of the beauty of their rugged province, and ready to fight to safeguard it from pollution.

A Canadian thinker, Marshall McLuhan of the University of Toronto, had become famous for declaring that the world was becoming a "global village," big and small at the same time, where everyone was linked together with everyone else. One place where the idea seemed easy to understand was the Sun Yat-sen Garden, the only classical Chinese garden outside China, which lay nestled amid the urban hustle of downtown Vancouver. The city's Asian-Canadian communities, once downtrodden minorities, had become a precious link between Canada and the Far East. Japan and Asia were surging forward in the world economy, and British Columbia schools put Asian culture and languages on the course of study.

In the 1970s, the combination of global pressures and regional claims made life hard for Canada's prime ministers. "I can lose. I just never do," said Pierre Trudeau boldly when someone asked him about elections. But he almost lost the election of 1972, and Joe Clark and the Conservative Party did beat him in 1979. Clark was a young unknown, and reporters nicknamed him "Joe Who?" He promised to make Canada "a community of communities," where every region would take charge of its own affairs, but his government lasted only nine months before Trudeau was back as prime minister.

Finally – in the middle of a snowstorm on February 29, 1984, the extra day of leap year – Pierre Trudeau decided he would retire. Except for John Diefenbaker's six years and Joe Clark's brief victory, the Liberal Party had held power in Ottawa since the 1930s. But in September 1984 the Progressive Conservatives were voted in and their new leader, Brian Mulroney, became Canada's nineteenth prime minister.

Lean and Mean

On October 5, 1984, the American space shuttle rocketed skyward on a pillar of flame. In minutes the shuttle was in orbit with Marc Garneau of Quebec City as one of the seven astronauts on board. Garneau, the first Canadian to see the earth from space, saw our vast country stretched out beneath him – seven times, in fact, as he crossed over it during that eight-day voyage. More than ever, Canada's future seemed linked with every place on the shrinking planet.

A month before Marc Garneau's flight, Brian Mulroney had become the prime minister of Canada. Mulroney came from a working-class, Irish-Canadian family in Baie Comeau, Quebec, on the north shore of the St. Lawrence River. He had been bilingual all his life, and, in both official languages, he loved to talk. By the time he became prime minister, he was using the telephone so much that his cronies all across the country joked that he had "black wire disease."

Brian Mulroney and his Progressive Conservative government promised to open Canada up to the world. At the end of the Second World War, Canada and the United States had been two rich countries in a poor, war-battered world. By the 1980s, however, Japan and the countries of Western Europe were racing to catch up – and even surpass – North America. In fact, Canada's continued prosperity could no longer be guaranteed in this fast-changing world. Prime Minister Mulroney said that Canada had to be "lean and mean" to survive. He meant cutting back on social services that many Canadians held dear, including trans-Canada passenger trains. The government sold Air Canada, the national airline, and Petro-Canada, the national oil company. Something else that vanished was the dollar bill. The dollar coin went into circulation in 1987; the last bills were printed two years later. Because of the image of a loon on the coin, Canadians nicknamed it the loonie, and when the two-dollar coin came along in 1996, it promptly became the toonie.

A satellite, just released by the "Canadarm," took this photo of the space shuttle in orbit. Astronaut Marc Garneau was the first Canadian to fly aboard the space shuttle.

In 1988 the Mulroney government negotiated and signed the Free Trade Agreement with the United States. Although Canadian companies and jobs that had been protected from American competition might vanish, the Progressive Conservatives were confident that, in the long run, the agreement would be good for the country. They said that Canada had to compete in the world marketplace and that free trade with the United States was the place to start.

The federal election that year was the most fiercely fought in recent years. Support in the country swung

Terry Fox

Lift, hop. Lift, hop. Lift, hop. Rocking back and forth between his one good leg and his artificial one, the young man ran on. He tried to ignore the pain as he slowly wore away the distance between St. John's, Newfoundland, and his destination at the Pacific Ocean.

Terry Fox of Port

Coquitlam, B.C., was nineteen when he lost his right leg to cancer in 1977. While he was recovering, he dreamed of doing something that would inspire other cancer sufferers, and raise money to fight the disease. In April 1980, he set out on his "Marathon of Hope" – a run all the way across Canada.

All that summer, the slim, curly-haired runner struggled on, running forty kilometres a day. Canada began to pay attention. Television cameras reported on Terry's progress and, before long, crowds were gathering to see him in each town he passed through. Moved by his courage, people began to donate to cancer research.

By September, when the Marathon of Hope reached the north shore of Lake Superior, Terry Fox had covered over 5300 kilometres. He was halfway home, and he had raised nearly $2 million. But there he had to stop. Cancer had returned, this time in his lungs. He could not run any more, and in less than a year Terry Fox was dead.

When they heard how his run had been halted, Canadians donated more than $25 million for cancer research. And marathons named for him still raise funds all over Canada. Canada has had many fine athletes, but few have touched the hearts of as many Canadians as Terry Fox.

back and forth, back and forth. Liberal leader John Turner and New Democratic Party leader Ed Broadbent swore that a free trade agreement would mean that Canada would be swallowed up by the United States. They each promised to "tear up" the deal if elected. Mulroney swore that the future of Canada depended on the agreement. Finally, when all the votes were in on November 21, 1988, Brian Mulroney and his Progressive Conservatives had been re-elected – not by a landslide, but with a comfortable majority. Free trade with the U.S. began on January 1, 1989. In the coming years, Canadians would complain when the United States refused to accept freely traded Canadian lumber, cattle, and other products, but free trade did lead to a great increase in Canadian exports to our American neighbours.

At the End of the Century

By the 1980s, electronic gadgets – from digital watches to microwave ovens – were taking over from the electric devices that had seemed so amazing in the 1950s. There had been computers since the '50s, but they had cost millions of dollars, filled whole rooms, and needed teams of experts to keep them going. By the 1980s, the microscopically-small silicon chip had made lap-size computers more powerful than the old room-filling machines. Computers came into classrooms, offices, and homes, and "user-friendly" programs made them easy to operate. Then, in the 1990s, came the Internet and the World Wide Web, linking home, school, or business computers to networks everywhere. Soon kids were connecting to their friends on the Net the way their parents had once done on the telephone and in letters, and they quickly discovered that computers could be used, not only for chatting and school projects, but for games, contests, and even shopping. By 1990, one Canadian home in four had a Nintendo system.

Everybody dances when the Caribana parade rolls through Toronto to celebrate Caribbean-Canadian culture.

Canada's sombre and spectacular War Museum on the banks of the Ottawa River opened in 2005. It was designed by architect Raymond Moriyama.

Canadians, like everyone everywhere, were getting news instantly and becoming more aware of human suffering and global inequality, of famines and natural disasters. Not only was news travelling fast, so were diseases like the terrifying new Acquired Immune Deficiency Syndrome (or AIDS), which first showed up in the early 1980s and spread rapidly around the world, killing millions.

The 1980s saw culture of all kinds flourishing in Canada. In 1980 the *Opéra de Montréal* was founded. This was the fifth opera company in Canada, adding to the growing number of musical societies like symphony orchestras and ballet companies. The slight, ethereal Evelyn Hart was the prima ballerina of the Royal Winnipeg Ballet. Cape Breton Islander Rita MacNeil had everyone in Canada step-dancing. The National Youth Orchestra, founded in 1960, could now say that one in three musicians in Canadian orchestras had come from the NYO, and also that NYO graduates were playing in orchestras all over the world. Ottawa boasted two handsome new landmarks in the 1980s: the new, tall, granite-and-glass National Art Gallery and the Canadian Museum of Civilization (the most visited museum in Canada), with its undulating outer walls. In 1997 the 12.9 kilometre Confederation Bridge linking Prince Edward Island to the New Brunswick mainland was opened. The ferry crossing, including lineups to get on board, had sometimes taken five or six hours, but now the drive over the bridge took ten minutes.

By the end of the century there were more than 30 million people in Canada, more than twice as many as

Prime Minister Jean Chrétien chats with Governor-General Adrienne Clarkson just before she reads her first Throne Speech in the Senate Chamber on Parliament Hill, October 12, 1999.

at the end of the Second World War. Immigrants were still coming to look for better jobs and for greater opportunities for their children. In 1978, hundreds of thousands of refugees had fled Vietnam after the war there, often risking their lives in small, crowded, sometimes leaky boats. Church groups and neighbourhoods had sponsored thousands of these "Boat People" and helped them settle into communities all across Canada. In the years that followed, famine, poverty, and other wars – in Uganda, Lebanon, Bosnia, Sri Lanka, and Haiti – brought more refugees to add to the Canadian mosaic.

As people of different races and customs mingled on buses, in stores, in schools, in work places, and in neighbourhoods, both old and new Canadians worked to break down walls of prejudice and fear. Canadians whose families had been in the country for generations struggled to understand new languages and accents, while new Canadians tried to speak an unfamiliar language and learn new ways. Minority communities proudly celebrated their members who were achieving

A new leader for the 1990s, Nellie Cournoyea became government leader in the Northwest Territories in 1991.

Canadian women have just won the 1999 Women's World Hockey Championship in Helsinki, Finland, and Geraldine Heaney (right) races to congratulate goalie Sami Joe Small.

success in Canada in every walk of life and every field of endeavour. At the same time, they were safeguarding the unique qualities and customs they had brought from their homelands. Radio and television stations in different languages began broadcasting across the country. Falafel, shawarma, tacos, and sushi, as well as Thai, Indian, and Vietnamese foods were becoming as popular as Chinese food, fish-and-chips, and pizza. Canada was becoming known around the world as a great experiment in multiculturalism.

The roles of men and women were changing too. It was becoming commonplace for women to be doctors, lawyers, and bus drivers, and no longer outlandish for them to be engineers, politicians, or construction workers, and more men became nurses and stay-at-home parents. Women were demanding action against violence to themselves and their children, working to improve health and child care, insisting on equal pay with men, and access to jobs and professions that had been closed to them. When Canada's constitution was brought home from Britain in 1982, women's organizations made sure that the Charter of Rights included Article 28, which guaranteed equality between women and men. At the last minute, politicians announced a change that would have allowed any government to ignore Article 28 whenever it chose to. Women's groups across the country organized a blizzard of protest telegrams, phone calls, and confrontations, and they forced the government to back down.

In 1981 a young hockey player named Justine Blaney waged her own fight against discrimination. She had earned a place on a Metro Toronto Hockey League team but she was forbidden to play because the rules forbade women on men's teams. She fought her case all the way to the Supreme Court of Canada and, in 1986, she won.

The Global Village

After forty long years, suddenly the Cold War was over, and the shape of global politics changed dramatically. All through those years, the West (led mostly by Western Europe and North America) and the Communist East (led by the Soviet Union and China) had opposed each other with relentless hostility and suspicion. Then, one by one, in rapid succession, the Communist governments in Eastern Europe began to collapse. Not only had these governments restricted the freedom of their citizens, they had been unable to ensure supplies of even such basic needs as food and housing. When Mikhail Gorbachev became leader of the Communist Party of the Soviet Union in 1984, he promised changes. Those economic and social changes went farther and faster than anyone could control.

Astronaut Roberta Bondar, a doctor and a pilot, trained for eight years for her flight into space in 1992.

On November 9, 1989, the Berlin Wall, the symbol of the division of the world into Communist East and Democratic West, was smashed open. It was an historic moment when the wall was finally opened for all to go through, and East Germany and West Germany were able to become one country again. Within two years, the flood of change swept away the mighty Soviet Union, and broke it into its separate parts. Russia, Latvia, Lithuania, Estonia, Belarus, Ukraine, and others were once again independent states. In the Peoples' Republic of China, the Communist Party held tightly onto its power. In June, 1989, government soldiers there killed hundreds of protesting students and workers in Tiananmen Square in the heart of Beijing. But for the sake of economic prosperity, even China began to relax some of its fierce control over the lives of its people, and rapid growth began to alter the lives of Chinese citizens even if their government remained unchanged.

While this was happening in China, many of the countries in Europe were planning to form the European Union, and by 1992, twenty-seven separate countries had open borders, many common policies,

and a single passport for all their citizens. Many of them
agreed to share a common currency called the Euro.
This was a happy, hopeful moment in modern history.
The threat of global nuclear war was fading; countries
were working together; world peace and prosperity
really seemed possible.

World peace was not to be. In the 1990s, savage
conflicts arose in Europe, in Africa, and in the Middle
East. Canadian troops served as peacekeepers in the
African nations of Somalia and Rwanda and on the Pacific
island of East Timor. In the Middle East, when Iraq
invaded its neighbour Kuwait, Canada joined the
United Nations forces to drive the Iraqi occupiers out.
When Yugoslavia broke apart and its people went to war
against each other, Canadian troops were there with
other United Nations forces, struggling first to bring
peace to the embattled new states of Bosnia-
Herzegovina and Croatia, and later flying combat
missions during Kosovo's struggle with Serbia.

War was not the whole story in the 1990s. By then,
electronic communication and supersonic jet travel
linked every spot in the world, and business was
conducted around the globe and around the clock. The
food we ate, the clothes we wore, and the toys we
played with might be produced by hand a few
kilometres away or might come from Paris, Bangkok, or
Beijing. The music of Africa and India blended with
home-grown western music to make exciting new
sounds in concert halls, on city streets, and on home
computers. Television used satellites to beam digital
images of a soccer match, a pop concert, or a war all
around the world. Tourists from everywhere went
everywhere; Japanese were as common on Prince
Edward Island and in Algonquin Park as Canadians were
in Greece or Jamaica.

Canada was part of this new global culture. In 1987,
wheelchair-bound athlete Rick Hansen completed a
40,000 km, round-the-world journey. The "Man in
Motion" had wheeled his chair along the Great Wall of

China, crossed Canada, Europe, and Asia, and raised millions of dollars for research and physiotherapy. By the time he completed his marathon in Vancouver, he had worn out eleven pairs of gloves and 117 wheelchair tires. "Dreams do come true," he said.

Canadian writers, visual artists, singers, and composers were becoming international celebrities. Stars like Quebec's singing sensation, Céline Dion, Vancouver rocker Bryan Adams, writers Alice Munro, Margaret Atwood, and Brian Doyle, opera singer Ben Heppner, and the brilliant young cellist Ofra Harnoy were delighting fans all over the world. In 1992, novelist Michael Ondaatje won Britain's prestigious Man Booker Prize for *The English Patient*. In 1986 John Polanyi had won the Nobel Prize for chemistry. (Polanyi's prize-winning subject was "infrared chemiluminescence," but he became almost better known for his passionate advocacy for peace and disarmament.) In the 1990s, Nobel science prizes went to two other Canadians, Michael Smith and Bertram Brockhouse.

The world was being "standardized" or "globalized" and not everyone was in favour of it. A lot of critics said that it was happening because a few giant, multi-national corporations were running the world to suit themselves, not people and not the environment. People in Africa and Latin America were growing poorer and more desperate, and their leaders campaigned for fair trade rules that would give them a chance at sharing in the world's prosperity. With rising costs along with rising taxes, even Canadians began to doubt whether they could continue to afford their high standard of living. During the 1990s, Preston Manning, a political crusader from Alberta, launched a new political party, the Reform Party, and he came to Ottawa on the rallying cry, "The West wants in!" Manning and his Reformers were heroes to those who believed governments should be smaller and expect people to provide more for themselves. Across Canada, provincial and local governments began to cut back both services

His spine broken in an accident, B.C. athlete Rick Hansen began his "Man in Motion" tour, circling the world in a wheelchair to raise funds for spinal-cord research. Here fans gather in Quebec City as he rolls through.

and taxes. More and more people had need of the growing number of food banks, and there was a rapid increase of homeless people on the streets of every town and city. Canadians began to worry that medical care, pensions, and even public services like libraries might not survive.

There was a greater worry than all of this, though, and not just in Canada. All around the world people were slowly becoming aware of what we humans had been doing to our planet and its environment. From earliest times, human beings have always made use of the earth's bounty with scarcely a thought for the cost. When the first European colonists arrived on this continent, they prospered by selling the resources of land and sea to Europe. Now, five hundred years later, fishers on the Grand Banks of Newfoundland were finding it harder and harder to make a living cod fishing. By 1992, catches were so small that the federal government had to ban cod fishing on the Banks to protect the fish from becoming extinct.

At the same time, acid rain was killing the blue lakes and the maple forests of Ontario. Prairie farmers were finding the rich topsoil on their land was losing its nutrients. British Columbians saw empty "clear-cut" patches spreading across their mountains and coasts as

When oil tankers go on the rocks, everyone who cares comes out to save the seabirds and water mammals. These rescuers are working on the west coast of Vancouver Island.

Floods rampaged through the streets of Chicoutimi, Quebec, in July 1996, and more than 10,000 of the city's 60,000 people had to flee from their homes.

loggers cut down the towering ancient forests. Native communities were devastated when game disappeared from their hunting territories. Around every city, garbage dumps were becoming garbage mountains as consumers continued to throw out disposable products. In the 1950s and '60s, it had seemed that Canadians could have everything they wanted. Now people were beginning to realize that the cost to the planet might really be too high.

First Nations and Distinct Societies

In September 1987, Pope John Paul II, the leader of the Roman Catholic Church, came to Fort Simpson in the Northwest Territories to visit the Dene nation. He said Mass wearing native robes of deerskin, and he led prayers in the Dene language. John Paul declared that Native Canadians had governed themselves and practiced their own faiths long before Europeans brought theirs to Canada. He praised their determination to protect their culture and prayed that Canada might become "a model for the world in upholding the dignity of Aboriginal people."

During the 1980s and 1990s the Native people of Canada, still the poorest minority in the country, were fighting harder than ever to regain control of their lives. Leaders like Georges Erasmus, a Dene from the Northwest Territories, and Ovide Mercredi, a Manitoba

Canadian rowing champion Silken Laumann fought bravely back from an accident that threatened to destroy her chance for an Olympic medal in 1992. The whole world cheered as sheer determination powered her to a bronze medal.

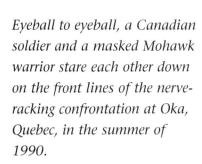

Eyeball to eyeball, a Canadian soldier and a masked Mohawk warrior stare each other down on the front lines of the nerve-racking confrontation at Oka, Quebec, in the summer of 1990.

Cree, became passionate spokesmen for their people, and their voices were being heard. Churches and governments responsible for the pain they had caused Native children at residential schools were beginning to make amends. Traditional elders began to regain their positions of influence, and younger Native people became lawyers, teachers, and social workers. Native entrepreneurs took over airlines, built fishing fleets, and opened craft co-ops. Ojibwa artist Norval Morrisseau impressed art lovers far and wide with his "Woodland" style of painting. Native architects, playwrights, actors, and musicians like Haida sculptor Bill Reid, Oneida actor Graham Greene, and Inuk singer Susan Aglukark were winning international fame.

As strength and confidence grew among Native nations, their leaders began to challenge the Canadian government to honour the promises, some centuries old, that had been made to them. The Cree of northern Quebec rallied international support to stop the damming of more of their rivers for electric power. The Haida of British Columbia, the Lubicon of Alberta, the Anishnabe of Ontario, the Innu of Labrador, and many others defended their traditional lands from loggers, miners, and other intruders. They wanted to practice their own beliefs and teach their children in their own ways – and they wanted their treaties respected.

In the summer of 1990, to protect land the Native people claimed at Oka and Kahnewaké, just outside

Montreal, Mohawk "Warriors" set up roadblocks and armed themselves with machine guns, ready to kill or die. The Quebec police, the RCMP, and then the Canadian army confronted the Warriors. People across the country feared a violent and tragic outcome. At last, the Warriors removed their barricades, but Natives everywhere declared that there would be more Okas unless Canada respected Native land and Native rights.

In the years that followed, judges in Canadian courts began to uphold Native claims to land and self-government. In British Columbia, where many Native nations had never signed treaties or surrendered their land or powers, the Gitk'san and Wet'su'wetan people of the Skeena Valley on the Northwest coast won an important court victory recognizing their rights. Soon after, the neighbouring Nisga'a people agreed to sign their first treaty with British Columbia and Canada. In the North, Inuit leaders began to plan the creation of a new territory where the Inuit would be a majority of the population. Nunavut, with its capital at Iqaluit on Baffin Island, became Canada's third territory on April 1, 1999, with Paul Okalik, an Inuk from Pangnirtung, as its first government leader.

Canadian governments only slowly conceded powers to Native Canadians, but Prime Minister Mulroney believed it was time to transfer powers from Ottawa to the provinces, and particularly to Quebec. In the referendum battle of 1980, Pierre Trudeau had promised Quebec a new kind of confederation. In 1987 Brian Mulroney set out to make the changes that first Quebec, and then the other provinces, had demanded. The Meech Lake Accord (named for the lake in the Gatineau Hills above Ottawa where the meeting took place) would give many powers once held by Ottawa to each province, and it declared that Quebec would have the powers of a "distinct society."

"It's a done deal," the prime minister said proudly when he presented the Accord to the Canadian people – but it wasn't. Each province had to approve the

Prime Minister Brian Mulroney had to fight hard to win the 1988 election. The big issue was his Canada–U.S. free trade agreement.

French President Jacques Chirac (left), a collector of Inuit art, was among the first foreign visitors to the new territory of Nunavut. Jean Chrétien and resident Rita Mike welcomed him to Pangnirtunq.

agreement within three years, and during those years, debate raged across the country, particularly over what exactly the words "distinct society" meant. As the deadline approached, the prime minister held another meeting, and again he thought he had a deal that would save the Accord. But the Meech Lake Accord had ignored the First Nations and they were determined not to be left out. In Manitoba, one of the provinces that had not yet approved the Accord, Elijah Harper, a Cree member of the Manitoba Legislature, said "No." Because not all the provinces had agreed to the Accord, it could not go ahead. On June 23, 1990, the Meech Lake Accord was dead.

Meech Lake had promised Quebec all the powers of a "distinct society," and at the last moment those powers had been snatched away. Many in the province decided that it was time to take charge of their own future – without the rest of Canada. Separatism, which had been declared dead back in 1980, gained new strength. Quebec premier Robert Bourassa gave the rest of Canada two years in which to make Quebec a new offer. For two stormy years, Canadians – in parliament and across the country – debated new constitutional

deals. The new solution was called the Charlottetown
Accord. This time all Canadians were to vote on the
Accord in a nation-wide referendum. After passionate
debates in kitchens, coffee shops, legislatures, and the
media, Canadians decided that the Accord was either
too much or too little. They voted it down in the fall
of 1992.

A few months later Brian Mulroney retired. The
Progressive Conservatives chose Kim Campbell from
Vancouver to be their new leader, making her Canada's
first woman prime minister – but not for long. In the
1993 election, the old, powerful Progressive
Conservative party was reduced to two seats in the
House of Commons. Jean Chrétien led his Liberals to
power. Preston Manning's Reform party held most of
the seats from the west, and Lucien Bouchard, who
spoke passionately for Quebec sovereignty, won fifty-
four seats for his new "Bloc Québécois."

Lucien Bouchard had once been Brian Mulroney's
federalist partner. Now he fought to divide the country.
On October 30, 1995, Quebec held a sovereignty
referendum. For the second time in fifteen years,
Quebeckers had to choose: Quebec or Canada? Just days
before the vote, tens of thousands of Canadians from
every province drove, flew, or rode the trains to
Montreal to say that they cared about having Quebec in
Confederation. Did they help? Did they make things
worse? The referendum vote was almost a tie. Separation
for Quebec had been rejected, but only by the merest
fraction. Lucien Bouchard left Ottawa to become
premier of Quebec in 1996.

Prime Minister Jean Chrétien rarely seemed worried.
Chrétien had come from a working-class family in
Shawinigan, Quebec, and he liked to call himself "the
little guy from Shawinigan." When he became prime
minister in 1993, nearly everyone underestimated him.
Although he loved to boast that the United Nations had
declared Canada the best country in the world to live
in, few saw him as a leader with vision. Yet he won

*Late in 1994, Bloc Québécois
leader Lucien Bouchard lost
one leg to a terrible illness.
After a remarkable – and brave
– recovery, he returned to his
crusade for Quebec sovereignty,
and he became Quebec's
premier in 1996.*

Days before the Quebec referendum of 1995, hundreds of thousands of passionate federalists carried the maple leaf through the streets of Montreal.

three elections in a row and served as prime minister for more than ten years.

In 1998, for the first time in thirty years, the government of Canada took in more money than it spent, giving hope to many that this would mean the end to rising debt and to cutbacks to public services.

The New Millennium

The twenty-first century arrived with exuberant celebrations all over the world – and one great worry. Was everything going to break down the instant 1999 became 2000? What would happen if the world's computers proved unable to read the new date? Y2K panic was everywhere (Y means year, 2K means 2000). The systems that ran bank machines, delivered heat, light, and electricity in our homes, offices, and supermarkets, made jet planes fly and trains run would all collapse. A lot of frightened people stocked up on non-perishable food and stored drinking water in huge plastic containers. The moment came. Computer systems changed over without a hitch and the new millennium began.

Fireworks burst over the Peace Tower on Parliament Hill to bring in the new millennium and the year 2000 in Ottawa.

But perhaps the new century really began on September 11, 2001. Early that morning, out of a clear blue sky, terrorists belonging to a little-known Islamic guerilla force called *al-Qaeda* flew hijacked airliners into the twin towers of New York's World Trade Center and into the Pentagon Building in Washington, D.C. The world watched in horror as two of the tallest buildings in the world crumbled and collapsed, taking the lives of

In 1995 thirteen-year-old Craig Kielburger of Thornhill, Ontario, won world-wide admiration for his campaign against the oppression of children in Asia.

Canadian soldiers of the International Security Assistance Force patrol the dusty, dangerous roads of southern Afghanistan in their armoured vehicles.

thousands of people with them, including twenty-four Canadians.

Five years later, on May 17, 2006, an armoured vehicle on a dusty, bare hillside near Kandahar, Afghanistan, was hit by a rocket-propelled grenade, and Canadian Forces Captain Nicola Goddard was among those killed. Captain Goddard was the first Canadian woman ever to die in combat. This Afghanistan mission was not peacekeeping. This grim, dangerous war against terrorism was one of the consequences of September 11.

In the countries of the Middle East and Asia where Islam is the dominant religion, many people had long felt oppressed by the power of western governments and western corporations. They feared their faith and way of life would be swallowed up by what they saw as an all-pervasive western culture. Some swore that only by imposing Islamic law and customs could Muslims hold to their own ways. The strictest among them preached *jihad*, which means struggle and war against non-believers. The jihadists of al-Qaeda had trained in Afghanistan when it was under the control of the radical *Taliban,* a strict Islamic regime. Soon after the attack on the World Trade Center, the United States helped Afghan forces to drive the Taliban and their al-Qaeda allies from power. Over thirty member-countries of the United Nations then sent combat troops to Afghanistan to defend the new government against insurgent Taliban and al-Qaeda fighters. Canada sent over 2000 troops as part of this mission. Another front in this confrontation between radical Islam and the West opened in March 2003, when a coalition of countries led by the United States invaded the Middle East nation of Iraq where the cruel dictator Saddam Hussein was said to be developing nuclear weapons. Canada stayed out of that war, which grew into a long and bloody struggle, but Canadian forces remained heavily engaged in Afghanistan. Captain Goddard was just one of thirty-seven Canadians killed in action in Afghanistan in 2006. This was the first armed conflict in which Canadians had been involved since the Korean War; until Afghanistan, our soldiers had been engaged solely in peacekeeping missions.

The wars were in Asia and the Middle East, but the conflict of cultures was everywhere, including Canada. Canadians take pride in being the most multicultural country in the world, but militant Muslim jihadists in other countries were starting to make quite a few people in Canada nervous. And while most Canadian Muslims were making vital contributions to Canadian society, there were radicals among them who believed that true Muslims should not accept the rule of western law, the equality of men and women, or the freedom of speech and behaviour. Nor were Muslim Canadians the only immigrant community in which some members were unhappy with Canadian openness. Immigrants and refugees continued to pour into Canada at the rate of 240,000 every year: from South America, the Middle East, India, Pakistan, Africa, China, and Japan. So many cultural differences among so many people can cause misunderstandings, hurt feelings, and sometimes even violence. Would Canadians resist the new immigrants' different traditions, beliefs, and ways of living? Would

As she prepares to open Parliament, Governor General Michaëlle Jean is attended by Stephen Harper (left), who became prime minister of Canada in 2006.

they tolerate young Muslim women wearing the headscarves called *hijabs*? Only time will tell. One sign that the newcomers could still thrive in Canada was the way Governor General Adrienne Clarkson, once a child immigrant from China, was succeeded in 2006 by Michaëlle Jean, an immigrant from Haiti. Many saw these two women as symbols of the success of Canada's diverse population.

There have been many changes in Canada since the year 2000, but some things have not changed. Canadian musicians – Shania Twain, Avril Lavigne, and The Arcade Fire – and filmmakers like Denys Arcand have been hits on the international stage. Canadians, always great winter athletes, continued to star on the ice in the first years of the new millennium. In the 2002 Winter Olympics at Salt Lake City, U.S.A., the Canadians buried a loonie at centre ice to inspire the men's and women's hockey teams. With Wayne Gretzky managing the men's team and Hayley Wickenheiser starring among the women, both teams won gold medals. At those games, the figure skating team of Jamie Salé and David Pelletier won gold after skating together for only six months. Canada cheered! Canadians cheered again in 2006, in Torino, Italy, for Brad Gushue's gold-winning curling team from Newfoundland and the dynamic Winnipeg speed skater Cindy Klassen, the "Woman of the Games," who ended the Olympics with five medals. In 2005, nineteen-year-old Sidney Crosby from Nova Scotia burst onto the NHL hockey scene. In his first season, he became the youngest player in history to score 100 points.

Prime Minister Jean Chrétien retired from office in 2003, undefeated after ten years in power. His successor, Paul Martin, was not so fortunate. In the early winter election of 2006, the Liberals were knocked out of power by Stephen Harper of Calgary, once an organizer of the Reform movement. He had become the leader of the now-united Reform and Conservative parties, and he became Canada's twenty-second prime minister.

What's so funny about the "Little Mosque"?

On Jan 9, 2007, the CBC's new television comedy sitcom, *Little Mosque on the Prairie*, drew worldwide attention. The show is about a group of Muslims in a small prairie community and how they do and don't get along with the old-time residents. In the tense times created by terrorist attacks, the Iraq war, and the conflict in Afghanistan, a comedy about how Muslims and non-Muslims get along took everyone by surprise. But in its first season, "Little Mosque" was immensely popular. Its creator and author, Zarqa Nawaz, is a Muslim writer and film-maker who lives in Regina and works hard to bring fun into her multicultural creations.

Canadian comedy thrived in many forms. Brent Butt's situation comedy *Corner Gas*, set in the fictional town of Dog River, Saskatchewan, became a hit for the CTV network. Standup comedians and satirists thrived on television and at events such as Montreal's annual Just For Laughs comedy festival. In 2003 YouTube videos leaked onto the Internet helped to build a worldwide fan base for Indo-Canadian comedian Russell Peters. He soon emerged as a global star.

Canadian actors Carlo Rota and Sitara Hewitt play father and daughter Yasir and Rayyan Hamoudi on Little Mosque on the Prairie.

It seemed like the right time for a prime minister from Calgary. Alberta had the most dynamic economy in Canada, based on its rich reserves of oil and other resources for an energy-hungry world. In the far north of the province, the huge industrial projects of the Athabasca oil sands, potentially one of the greatest energy sources in the world, attracted workers from all across Canada. With Newfoundland's cod fishery still closed, some Newfoundland towns had more of their inhabitants in Fort McMurray (Fort McMoney, some

The Poppy Quarter

In 2004, it was something special to find a flash of crimson on the coins you got in your change. The colourful coin was a special commemorative issue, a twenty-five cent piece with a red poppy in the centre, circulated by the Canadian Mint that year to salute Canada's war dead and our veterans. But the next year, several visiting American army contractors, finding these "strange looking coins" in their pockets, reported them to the U.S. Department of Defense. That department briefly suspected that the poppies were tiny radio frequency transmitters, and the coins were spy money, planted on the contractors in order to spy on them.

called it), the capital of the region around the oil sands, than they had at home. Calgary, the financial capital of western Canada and Canada's fastest-growing city, had become a gleaming modern metropolis back in the 1980s. In 1988, one of the most successful Winter Olympics ever held symbolized how Calgary was taking its place among the great Canadian cities.

In many ways, the world in the twenty-first century was more united, more prosperous, and more able to fill the aspirations of its people than ever before. At the same time, there was the war in the Middle East, widespread global poverty, the AIDS epidemic, and underdevelopment in Africa. And no worry loomed larger than the threat to the earth's environment. In the last decades of the twentieth century, the world had slowly begun to accept that the way humankind was polluting the environment posed a very real threat to life on earth. Environmentalists struggled to get people to cut down their own contributions to pollution and to

"reduce, reuse, and recycle." They campaigned for a
system that could provide the riches Canadians
expected without leaving our world unlivable.

Some progress had been made. Agreements had
been reached to fight the acid rain that had been killing
the lakes and forests of the industrialized world. In the
Montreal Protocol of 1987, the world agreed to cut back
on the chemicals that had been destroying the ozone
layer that shields our planet. Slowly, though,
understanding began to dawn about a much greater
problem: all the industrial activity of humankind was
pumping carbon dioxide and other "greenhouse gases"
into our atmosphere, and steadily, even rapidly,
warming the earth's temperature. The words "global
warming" suddenly became part of everyday language.

In 1997 in Kyoto, Japan, world leaders negotiated a
new United Nations agreement, the Kyoto Protocol, to
slow down the release of the carbon dioxide and other
greenhouse gases that were heating the atmosphere.
Canada approved the Kyoto Protocol in 2002, but
approval did not lead to action; there was no reduction
in emissions. When Stephen Harper and his
Conservatives formed the government in 2006, they
declared that Canada's Kyoto commitments were
impossible to meet – and perhaps unnecessary. Now,
debates and arguments continue in Canada and in the
rest of the world. How much action should we take? If
none is taken, will our coastal cities be flooded by rising
sea water, our farms scorched by searing droughts?
Already Canadian winters are milder than they have
ever been, summers hotter.

While debates heat up in governments, ordinary
Canadians have started taking matters into their own
hands. Often it has been kids, made aware of the
dangers to the environment from television, school, the
Internet, and the books they read, who have persuaded
their parents to pay attention to what they buy, how
much electricity they use, and how much they drive
their cars. Incandescent light bulbs are giving way to

To honour his work as an environmental activist, David Suzuki was named a Companion of the Order of Canada in 2006.

new energy-efficient fluorescent ones. A few people are heating their houses with solar panels. More are riding bicycles, taking buses, or driving fuel-efficient small cars. Some are driving hybrid cars run by a combination of electricity and gas or diesel fuel. Many people now take their groceries home in boxes or cloth bags, avoiding the non-biodegradable plastic. They look for vegetables grown locally and not sprayed with pesticides, or they grow their own. The new century has brought new ways to understand the country, the environment, and the wider world we live in.

At the start of the 1900s, Prime Minister Wilfrid Laurier had predicted that the twentieth century would be Canada's. At the start of the twenty-first century, Canada had grown into one of the safest, most prosperous, most democratic, and most respected countries in the world. Life was good for a very large number of citizens. Yet French and English Canadians still distrusted each other, and many still felt excluded from the running of the country. Each region had claims and complaints. Minority groups wanted recognition for their languages, their cultural traditions, and their political beliefs. Business leaders warned that the country was falling behind in the fierce competition of global trade. Was there a unique and distinctive Canadian style? Sometimes it was hard to believe there had been a national dream, a feeling that Canada was something special in the world.

In 1867, D'Arcy McGee had looked forward to "a new nationality" emerging from Confederation, and John A. Macdonald had imagined "one people." But at the dawn of the twenty-first century, Canada remains many peoples, many communities. The Canadian experiment had been to build a nation out of many nations and to find a way for them to live in harmony with each other and with this northern land. It has never been easy. It is still hard.

Northern Voyagers

I N JULY 1986, JEFF MACINNIS, A 23-YEAR-OLD STUDENT from Toronto, and Mike Beedell, an Arctic photographer from Ottawa, sailed out of the Mackenzie River delta to challenge the Northwest Passage.

There is no easy way through the Northwest Passage, but for MacInnis and Beedell the voyage would be exceptionally daring. They were setting out with sails and paddles alone, aboard a bright yellow catamaran less than six metres long. *Perception* had no motor, no cabin, and no shelter, just twin hulls of yellow fibreglass and a single mast. The pair looked as if they should be sailing for fun on a pond by a cottage, not steering out into treacherous Arctic waters.

Since 1906, when Roald Amundsen's *Gjoa* first completed the passage, many other adventurers have challenged the Northwest Passage. The idea of the passage has never ceased casting its spell. In the 1970s, songwriter Stan Rogers put it into words in these lines from his song "Northwest Passage":

> . . . for just one time, I would take the Northwest Passage
> To find the hand of Franklin reaching for the Beaufort Sea
> Tracing one warm line through a land so wide and savage
> And make a Northwest Passage to the sea

Mike Beedell and Jeff MacInnis haul the Perception across ice on King William Island.

Until his death at age thirty-three in an airplane accident, folksinger and writer Stan Rogers touched audiences with his music of farmers, sailors, and fishing towns.

Westward from the Davis Strait, 'tis there 'twas said
  to lie
The sea-route to the Orient for which so many died
Seeking gold and glory, leaving weathered broken
  bones
And a long-forgotten lonely cairn of stones.

Even in the Far North, MacInnis and Beedell saw
how human beings had overcome nature. Aircraft
roared low over their heads, and powerful radios kept
them in touch with the world. The two voyagers passed
artificial islands built around oil wells, and they visited
radar stations ready to give a few minutes' warning of
any nuclear attack. Franklin and Frobisher never knew
such wonders – or the threat of such horrors.

In their Northwest Passage adventure, MacInnis and
Beedell did not try to overpower the North. When the
Arctic wind blew against them, they stopped. When it
died, they paddled by hand. Sometimes they dragged
their boat, metre by painful metre, across jagged and
rolling floes of ice. Just as often, the ice drove them back
or sent them dashing for refuge ashore. Yet, when wind

and ice allowed, they sailed on to complete their voyage. Over three exciting summers, *Perception* carried them 3500 kilometres, from Inuvik at the Mackenzie River delta to Atlantic tidewater at Pond Inlet on Baffin Island.

MacInnis and Beedell were close not only to nature but to history, to thousands of years of Arctic adventurers, all the way. Only *Perception*'s thin hulls and the men's insulated, watertight suits kept them from the killing cold. Razor-edged ice ripped their suits and froze their fingers. Seals and beluga whales bobbed up around them, and sometimes they were stalked by polar bears. They saw history in the remains of Inuit campsites and at the graves of men who had sailed with Sir John Franklin in 1845.

"Nature must be ridden, not driven" became the motto of *Perception*'s voyage. When all Canadians can learn that lesson, the new century will bring adventures beyond our imaginings. Perhaps our children's children will see a Canadian land as fresh and beautiful and full of dreams as the land the first people knew a hundred centuries ago. There are northern passages, yet uncrossed, awaiting them.

The scenic Mackenzie River delta, where the North's greatest river flows into the Arctic Sea.

Chronology

About 75 million years ago Dinosaurs live in steamy forests and warm seas that cover much of what we now call Canada.

About 20 000 years ago The first human inhabitants of North America probably cross from Siberia by land bridge as the last Ice Age draws to a close.

About 1000 years ago Native people of southern Ontario begin to plant and harvest corn. The Thule people – ancestors of the Inuit – migrate east across Arctic Canada.

About 1000 years ago Leif Ericsson's first voyage to Vinland. A Norse colony is established in Vinland, but lasts only a couple of years.

About 600 years ago Five Iroquois nations form the powerful Confederacy of the Longhouse.

1497, 1498 John Cabot (Giovanni Caboto) of Genoa makes two voyages for England to the fishing grounds off Newfoundland.

1534 Jacques Cartier explores the coasts of Newfoundland, Prince Edward Island, and New Brunswick. He lands on the Gaspé Peninsula and claims the land for France.

1535 Cartier journeys up the St. Lawrence to the Native settlements of Stadacona and Hochelaga. He gives Canada its name (from the Indian word *kanata*, meaning "village").

1576 Martin Frobisher journeys as far as Frobisher Bay, Baffin Island, on the first of three voyages in search of the Northwest Passage.

1583 Sir Humphrey Gilbert visits Newfoundland and claims it for England.

1604 Pierre Du Gua de Monts and Samuel de Champlain establish a colony in Nova Scotia. Marc Lescarbot starts the first library and first French school for Native people, and in 1606 produces the first play staged in Canada. After Lescarbot returns to France, he writes the first history of Canada.

1608 Samuel de Champlain founds a permanent French colony at Quebec.

1610–1611 Explorer Henry Hudson is set adrift by his mutinous crew in Hudson Bay.

1615 The first Roman Catholic missionaries try to convert the Native people to Christianity.

1616 Champlain completes eight years of exploration, travelling as far west as Georgian Bay. The French and Hurons form an alliance.

1617 Louis and Marie Hébert and their children become the first French settlers to farm land in New France.

1630s The first French schools are founded in Quebec by religious orders.

1642 Ville-Marie (Montreal) is founded by Paul de Maisonneuve.

1645 The Hôtel-Dieu Hospital in Ville-Marie, founded by Jeanne Mance, is completed.

1649 War between the Huron and Iroquois confederacies leads to the destruction of the Huron nation. The Iroquois begin raids on New France.

1663 King Louis XIV decides to rebuild New France. He sends a governor and troops to protect the colony, an intendant (Jean Talon) to administer it, and settlers to increase its population.

1670 The English king grants a charter to the Hudson's Bay Company, giving it exclusive trading rights to vast territory drained by rivers that flow into Hudson Bay.

1682 René-Robert Cavelier de La Salle reaches the mouth of the Mississippi, and claims for France all the land through which the river and its tributaries flow.

Early 1700s Horses come to the northern plains, and the region's Native peoples become nations on horseback.

1713 A peace treaty forces France to turn over Newfoundland and Acadia to Britain. The French begin construction of Louisbourg, strongest fortress in North America, on Cape Breton Island.

1726 The first English school in Newfoundland is established, known as "the school for poor people."

1743 Louis-Joseph, son of Pierre de La Vérendrye, explores westward in search of the "Western Sea," crossing the plains almost to the Rocky Mountains.

1749 The British found Halifax as a naval and military post; about 3000 people settle there in one year.

March 25, 1752 First issue of the *Halifax Gazette*, Canada's first newspaper.

1755 The expulsion of the Acadians by the British begins: 6000–10 000 Acadians driven from their homes.

1756–1763 The Seven Years' War between Great Britain and France, fought partly in their North American colonies: ***July 8, 1758*** French troops, under the command of Louis-Joseph de Montcalm, win victory over the British at Carillon (Ticonderoga). ***July 26, 1758*** The British capture Louisbourg from the French. ***September 13, 1759*** At the Battle of the Plains of Abraham, Quebec falls to the British. Both commanders, Wolfe and Montcalm, are killed. ***September 8, 1760*** New France surrenders to the British. ***1763*** New France becomes a British colony called Quebec.

1763 Alliance of Native nations under Pontiac, chief of the Ottawa, makes war on the British, seizing many forts and trading posts.

1769 Prince Edward Island, formerly part of Nova Scotia, becomes separate British colony.

1770–1772 Samuel Hearne, guided by Chipewyan leader Matonabbee, explores the Coppermine and Slave rivers and Great Slave Lake and is the first white man to reach the Arctic Ocean overland.

1773 Scottish settlers reach Pictou, Nova Scotia, aboard the *Hector*.

1774 Quebec Act is passed by British Parliament, recognizing the French Canadians' right to preserve their language, religion, and civil law.

1775–1783 The American Revolution gains independence from Great Britain for the Thirteen Colonies. The people of Quebec, Nova Scotia, and Prince Edward Island decide against joining the revolution.

December 31, 1775 American invaders under General Montgomery assault Quebec. The city is under siege until spring, when British reinforcements drive the Americans away.

1776 The fur traders of Montreal band together in the North West Company to compete with the traders of the Hudson's Bay Company.

1778 Captain James Cook explores the Pacific Coast from Nootka (Yuquot Cove) to the Bering Strait.

1783 Immigration of 40 000 United Empire Loyalists from the Thirteen Colonies. Most settle in Nova Scotia, Quebec, and New Brunswick (established as a colony separate from Nova Scotia in 1784). Three thousand Black Loyalists settle near Shelburne, Nova Scotia.

1784 After helping the British during the American Revolution, the Iroquois are given two land grants. Thayendanegea (Joseph Brant) settles his followers at the Six Nations Reserve, near Brantford.

1791 Quebec is divided into two colonies, Upper and Lower Canada, each with its own Assembly.

1792, 1793, 1794 Captain George Vancouver makes summer voyages to explore the coasts of mainland British Columbia and Vancouver Island.

1793 By canoe and on foot, Alexander Mackenzie crosses the Rocky Mountains and the Coast Range, reaching the Pacific Ocean on July 22.

1793 York (now Toronto) founded by John Graves Simcoe, lieutenant-governor of Upper Canada.

1803 First paper mill established in Lower Canada, producing paper from cloth rags.

1808 Simon Fraser travels the Fraser River for 1360 km to reach the Pacific Ocean on July 2.

1811 Lord Selkirk plans a settlement of Highland Scots in Red River area, near present site of Winnipeg. First settlers arrive at Hudson Bay in the fall of 1811.

1812–1814 The War of 1812, between the United States and Britain: ***August 16, 1812*** Detroit surrenders to British general Isaac Brock and Tecumseh, leader of the Native nations allied to Britain. ***October 13, 1812*** Brock is killed during the Battle of Queenston Heights. ***June 22, 1813*** Laura Secord overhears American troops planning an attack, and walks 30 km, crossing enemy lines, to warn Colonel James FitzGibbon. Two days later, the Americans are ambushed and surrender to FitzGibbon. ***October 5, 1813*** Tecumseh dies during

the British defeat at Moraviantown. ***December 24, 1814*** The Treaty of Ghent officially ends the war.

June 6, 1829 Shawnandithit, the last of the Beothuks, dies at about age twenty-eight in St. John's, Newfoundland.

1830 Escaped slaves Josiah and Charlotte Henson and their children journey north from Maryland to Canada. The Hensons later help found a community of ex-slaves called Dawn, near Dresden, Ontario.

1832 The Rideau Canal, built by Colonel John By, opens; the community of Bytown (later Ottawa) grows out of the camp for the canal workers.

1836 The first railway in Canada opens, running from La Prairie to St. John's, Quebec.

1837 Rebellions in Upper and Lower Canada are put down by government troops. The rebel leaders, Louis-Joseph Papineau of Lower Canada and William Lyon Mackenzie of Upper Canada, are forced to flee.

1838 Lord Durham comes to Canada as governor. He recommends that the governments of the colonies should be chosen by the people's elected representatives.

1840 *Britannia* – the first ship of the Cunard Line, founded by Samuel Cunard of Halifax – arrives in Halifax harbour with transatlantic mail.

1841 The Act of Union unites Upper and Lower Canada (which became Canada West and Canada East) into the Province of Canada, under one government, with Kingston as capital.

1842 Charles Fenerty of Sackville, New Brunswick, discovers a practical way to make paper from wood pulp. Today the pulp and paper industry is Canada's largest manufacturing industry, and Canada exports more pulp and paper than any other country in the world.

1843 James Douglas of the Hudson's Bay Company founds Victoria on Vancouver Island.

1845 Sir John Franklin and his crew disappear in the Arctic while seeking the Northwest Passage.

1846 Geologist and chemist Abraham Gesner of Nova Scotia invents kerosene oil and becomes the founder of the modern petroleum industry.

1851 Canada's first postage stamp is issued, a three-penny stamp with a beaver on it.

1856 Timothy Eaton opens his first general store, in Kirkton, Ontario. Thirteen years later he opens a store at the corner of Queen and Yonge in Toronto.

1857 Queen Victoria chooses Ottawa as the new capital of the United Province of Canada.

1858 Gold is discovered in the sandbars of the Fraser River. Some twenty thousand miners rush to the area, and it comes under British rule as the colony of British Columbia.

1859 The French acrobat Blondin crosses Niagara Falls on a tightrope. On later tightrope walks, he crosses the falls on stilts, blindfolded, and with his feet in a sack.

1864 Confederation conferences in Charlottetown, Prince Edward Island, September 1–9, and in Quebec, October 10–29. Delegates hammer out the conditions for union of British North American colonies.

March 29, 1867 The British North America Act is passed by Britain's Parliament, providing for Canada's Confederation.

July 1, 1867 Confederation: New Brunswick, Nova Scotia, Quebec, and Ontario form the Dominion of Canada, and John A. Macdonald becomes the first prime minister.

1867 Emily Stowe, the first woman doctor in Canada, begins to practise medicine in Toronto.

1869 The Métis of Red River rebel, under Louis Riel, after their region is purchased by Canada from the Hudson's Bay Company.

July 15, 1870 Manitoba joins Confederation. The new province was much smaller than today's Manitoba.

1870 As buffalo become scarce, the last tribal war is fought on the Prairies between the Cree and the Blackfoot over hunting territories.

July 20, 1871 British Columbia joins Confederation.

May 1873 American whisky traders kill fifty-six Assiniboine in the Cypress Hills of the southern Prairies. The North-West Mounted Police (later the RCMP) is formed to keep order in the new Canadian territories.

1873 Prime Minister Sir John A. Macdonald resigns as a result of scandal over the partial financing of the Conservative election campaign by the Canadian Pacific Railway Company.

July 1, 1873 Prince Edward Island joins Confederation.

August 1876 Scottish-born Alexander Graham Bell, who has been working on the invention of the telephone since 1874, makes the world's first long-distance call, from Brantford to Paris, Ontario.

1879 The first organized games of hockey, using a flat puck, are played by McGill University students in Montreal. Before this, hockey-like games have been played on ice with a ball.

1880 Britain transfers the Arctic, which it claims to own, to Canada, completing Canada's modern boundaries – except for Newfoundland and Labrador.

1884 A system of international standard time and official time zones, advocated by Canadian engineer Sir Sandford Fleming, is adopted.

1885 The Métis North-West Rebellion is led by Louis Riel and Gabriel Dumont. After early victories for the rebels, the rebellion is crushed by troops who arrive on the newly built railway.

November 7, 1885 The last spike of the Canadian Pacific Railway main line is driven at Craigellachie, B.C. The next year, Vancouver is founded as the railway's western terminus.

1891 The City of Toronto establishes the first Children's Aid Society in Canada.

1893 Lord Stanley, the governor general, donates the Stanley Cup as a hockey trophy.

1896 Gold is discovered in the Klondike. By the next year, 100 000 people are rushing to the Yukon in the hope of getting rich.

1899–1902 The Boer War in South Africa is fought between Dutch Afrikaners (Boers) and the British. Seven thousand Canadian volunteers fight on the British side.

September 1, 1905 Saskatchewan and Alberta join Confederation. Immigrants rush to settle on the plains, mainly as wheat farmers.

1906 Norwegian Roald Amundsen, in the schooner *Gjoa*, finds his way through the Northwest Passage to the Pacific.

1907 Tom Longboat, an Onondaga from the Six Nations Reserve and a world champion distance runner, wins the Boston Marathon in record time. In 1906 he won a 12-mile (almost 20 km) race against a horse.

1908 *Anne of Green Gables*, by Lucy Maud Montgomery, is published. In the next ninety years the book sells more than a million copies, is made into a television movie, and becomes a popular musical.

1909 The first powered, heavier-than-air flight in Canada is made by J.A.D. McCurdy in the *Silver Dart*. The biplane flew almost a kilometre.

1909 The first Grey Cup game; the University of Toronto football team defeats Toronto Parkdale. A trophy has been donated by the governor general, Earl Grey.

1911 A proposal for free trade between the United

States and Canada is rejected in a fiercely contested general election. The Liberal government, under Wilfrid Laurier, is replaced by a Conservative government led by Sir William Borden.

1913 Vilhjalmur Stefansson leads a Canadian expedition to the Arctic, and explores the North by deliberately drifting on ice floes.

1914–1918 The First World War. Britain declares war on Germany on behalf of the British Empire, including Canada. *April 22–May 25, 1915* Battle of Ypres (Belgium). The first major battle fought by Canadian troops. They stand their ground against poison-gas attacks. *April 9–14, 1917* Battle of Vimy Ridge (France). A Canadian victory, at cost of more than 10 000 killed or wounded. *October 26–November 7, 1917* Passchendaele (Belgium). A Canadian victory, at the cost of more than 15 000 casualties. Nine Victoria Crosses are awarded to Canadians. *1917* Flying ace Billy Bishop of Owen Sound, Ontario, wins the Victoria Cross for attacking a German airfield single-handed.

November 26, 1917 The National Hockey League is established in Montreal.

The original teams are: Montreal Canadiens, Montreal Wanderers, Ottawa Senators, and Toronto Arenas.

1917 Sir William Borden leads a unionist coalition, which combines support by Conservatives and western Liberals, into a wartime election against the Laurier Liberals. Borden wins.

December 6, 1917 A French munitions ship explodes in Halifax harbour, flattening the city, killing 1600, and injuring 9000.

1918 Women win the right to vote in federal elections.

May 15–June 25, 1919 The Winnipeg General Strike. A strike in the building and metal trades spreads to other unions, and 30 000 workers stop work, crippling the city.

August 1919 Following the death of Laurier, William Lyon Mackenzie King is chosen to be leader of the Liberal Party.

1920 The Group of Seven artists hold their first exhibition, in Toronto.

1921 Agnes Macphail of Owen Sound, Ontario, becomes the first woman elected to the House of Commons, in the first election since women gained the vote.

1923 The Nobel Prize for Medicine is awarded to

doctors Frederick Banting and J.J.R. Macleod. Along with Dr. Charles Best and others, Banting discovered insulin as a treatment for diabetes.

1927 The first government old-age pension pays up to $20 per month.

July 1, 1927 To celebrate Canada's Diamond jubilee (sixtieth birthday), the first coast-to-coast radio broadcast is made.

1928 At the first Olympics in which women may compete, a Canadian women's six-member track team wins one bronze, two silver, and two gold medals.

1929 England's Privy Council rules that women are indeed "persons," and therefore can be appointed to the Canadian Senate. The next year, Cairine Wilson becomes Canada's first woman senator.

October 29, 1929 North American stock markets crash and the Great Depression begins.

1930 R.B. Bennett leads the Conservative Party to victory over William Lyon Mackenzie King's Liberals as the country is plunged into the Great Depression.

November 2, 1936 The Canadian Broadcasting Corporation is established.

April 1, 1939 Trans-Canada Airlines (later Air Canada) makes the first scheduled passenger flight from Vancouver to Montreal.

1939–1945 The Second World War. After Germany invades Poland and Britain declares war, Canada declares war as well. ***December 7, 1941*** The Japanese attack the U.S. naval base at Pearl Harbor, in Hawaii, and Canada declares war on Japan. ***December 1941*** The Fall of Hong Kong. More than 500 Canadians die in battle or of starvation and ill-treatment in Japanese prison camps. ***1942*** Twenty-two thousand Japanese Canadians are rounded up by RCMP and placed in work camps until after the war. ***August 19, 1942*** In a disastrous raid on Dieppe, France, 900 out of 5000 Canadians are killed and almost 2000 are taken prisoner. ***May–October 1942*** German submarines in the Gulf of St. Lawrence sink twenty-three Allied ships, with a loss of 258 lives. The gulf is then closed to ocean shipping until 1944. ***July 1943*** Canadian troops invade Sicily and, with other Allied troops, fight their way north through Italy. They reach Rome on June 4, 1944. ***June 6, 1944 (D day)*** Canadian troops, along with British and Americans, land successfully on the coast of France and begin to drive the Germans back.

July 1941 The first national unemployment-insurance program comes into operation.

1945 Family-allowance payments begin. All families receive a monthly sum for each child under sixteen who is in school.

February 1947 Prospectors strike oil in Leduc, Alberta, beginning Alberta's oil boom.

March 31, 1949 Newfoundland and Labrador join Confederation as the tenth province.

1949 William Lyon Mackenzie King, Canada's longest-serving prime minister, retires at the age of 74.

1950–1954 The Korean War. Twenty-seven thousand Canadians serve and more than 1600 are killed or wounded.

1950 Inuit win the right to vote in federal elections.

1952 Vincent Massey becomes the first Canadian-born governor general since Pierre Rigaud de Vaudreuil governed New France.

September 6, 1952 The first Canadian scheduled TV broadcast.

September 9, 1954 Marilyn Bell, age sixteen, is the first person to swim Lake Ontario.

1957 Lester Pearson wins the Nobel Peace Prize for proposing a United Nations peacekeeping force to prevent war over control of the Suez Canal.

1957 John George Diefenbaker leads the Conservative Party to decisive victory over Louis St. Laurent's Liberals in a federal election, winning more seats in the House of Commons than any party has before.

October 23, 1958 The Springhill Mining Disaster. Shifting rock kills seventy-four coal miners. Some of the survivors are trapped for eight days before being rescued.

June 26, 1959 Queen Elizabeth II and U.S. President Dwight Eisenhower officially open the St. Lawrence Seaway, which lets ocean vessels reach the Great Lakes.

1960 Native people living on reserves get the right to vote in federal elections.

1960 Social changes and a new government in Quebec lead to the beginning of Quebec's "Quiet Revolution." Stirrings of interest in independence for Quebec soon follow.

1962 Saskatchewan is the first province to have medical insurance covering doctors' bills. In 1966, Parliament passes legislation to establish a national medicare program. By 1972, all provinces and territories have joined the program.

September 29, 1962 The first Canadian satellite, *Alouette I*, is launched by the American space agency.

1963 The FLQ, a terrorist group dedicated to revolution to establish an independent Quebec, explodes bombs in Montreal.

February 15, 1965 Canada gets a new red-and-white, maple leaf flag.

1967 Canada celebrates a hundred years of Confederation. Across the country, communities sponsor centennial projects. In Ottawa, on July 1, Queen Elizabeth II cuts a giant birthday cake.

April–October 1967 Expo 67, the Montreal world's fair, attracts more than 55 million visitors.

1968 René Lévesque founds the Parti Québécois, with the goal of making Quebec a "sovereign" (independent) state "associated" with Canada.

1968 Pierre Elliott Trudeau succeeds Lester Pearson as prime minister and leader of the Liberal Party. "Trudeaumania" sweeps the country in the subsequent federal election.

1970 Voting age lowered from twenty-one to eighteen.

1970 The October Crisis. After the FLQ kidnaps a Quebec government minister and a British trade commissioner, Prime Minister Trudeau invokes the War Measures Act, which allows Canadians to be arrested and held without being charged.

1971 Gerhard Herzberg of Ottawa wins the Nobel Prize for Chemistry.

1976 René Lévesque and the Parti Québécois are elected in Quebec.

1976 Wayne Gretzky, age seventeen, plays hockey for the Edmonton Oilers; he is the youngest person in North America playing a major-league sport.

April 12, 1980 Terry Fox begins his cross-country run, the "Marathon of Hope." On September 1, he is forced to stop the run when his cancer returns.

May 15, 1980 Quebec voters reject "sovereignty-association" in favour of renewed Confederation.

November 1981 First flight of the Canadian Remote Manipulator System (Canadarm) on the space shuttle. The highly computerized 15m arm can be operated from inside the shuttle to release, rescue, and repair satellites.

November 5, 1981 The federal government and every province except Quebec reach agreement for patriating the Canadian constitution (bringing it to Canada from Great Britain).

April 17, 1982 Canada gets a new Constitution Act, including a Charter of Rights and Freedoms.

May 14, 1984 Jeanne Sauvé is Canada's first woman governor general.

1984 At the Summer Olympics in Los Angeles, Canada wins its greatest-ever number of gold medals: ten, including two for swimmer Alex Baumann.

October 5, 1984 Astronaut Marc Garneau, aboard the U.S. space shuttle *Challenger*, becomes the first Canadian in space.

March 21, 1985 Wheelchair athlete Rick Hansen leaves Vancouver on a round-the-world "Man in Motion" tour to raise money for spinal-cord research and wheelchair sports.

1986 John Polanyi of Toronto is co-winner of the Nobel Prize for Chemistry.

May–October 1986 Expo 86, the Vancouver world's fair, attracts more than 20 million visitors.

April 30, 1987 Ten provincial premiers and Prime Minister Brian Mulroney agree to the Meech Lake Accord, which would make large changes to Canada's Constitution and address Quebec's concerns. Parliament and the legislatures of all provinces have three years to accept the Accord. It dies in June 1991, when both Newfoundland and Manitoba refuse to endorse it.

February 13–28, 1988 The Calgary Winter Olympics. Canada wins two silver medals (Brian Orser and Elizabeth Manley, for figure skating) and three bronze medals.

January 1, 1989 After a federal election fought over the issue of free trade, the free-trade agreement between Canada and the United States comes into effect, gradually ending controls on trade and investment between the two countries.

December 2, 1989 Audrey McLaughlin becomes the first woman leader of a federal party – the New Democratic Party.

April 1990 The federal government settles a land

claim with the Inuit that will give them 350 000 square km of territory in the North, to be called Nunavut.

Summer 1990 A land dispute causes a 78-day armed confrontation between Mohawks and the army on a reserve near Oka, Quebec.

January–February 1991 War in the Persian Gulf. Canada sends three warships, twenty-six fighter jets, and 2400 people to the Persian Gulf as part of a United Nations effort to force Iraqi troops to withdraw from Kuwait.

January 22, 1992 Dr. Roberta Bondar becomes the first Canadian woman in space, aboard the U.S. space shuttle *Discovery*.

August 28, 1992 Canadian leaders adopt the Charlottetown Accord to reform Canada's constitution, but in a national referendum in October, Canadians reject it.

October 24, 1992 Toronto's Blue Jays became the first Canadian team to win baseball's World Series.

1993 Canada, with Kurt Browning (gold), Elvis Stojko (silver), and Isabelle Brasseur and Lloyd Eisler (gold), has its best skating World Championship since 1962.

June 25, 1993 Kim Campbell, the new Conservative party leader, becomes Canada's first female prime minister, but in October, Jean Chrétien's Liberals win the general election.

1994 The North American Free Trade Agreement (NAFTA) comes into effect, linking Canada, the United States, and Mexico in a new economic partnership.

September 15, 1994 Separatist Jacques Parizeau becomes the premier of Quebec.

1995 "Turbot war" erupts when Canada arrests a Spanish ship in a bid to prevent European fleets from over-harvesting Newfoundland fish stocks.

1995 Donovan Bailey becomes "the world's fastest man" when he breaks the record for the 100-metre race.

October 30, 1995 Quebec votes in a referendum on sovereignty and the federalists win a razor-thin victory.

January 29, 1996 Lucien Bouchard is sworn in as the new premier of Quebec.

May 19, 1996 Astronaut Marc Garneau makes his second trip into space.

1996 Lucien Bouchard becomes leader of the

separatist Parti Québécois and premier of Quebec.

Astronaut Marc Garneau makes his second trip into space.

Donovan Bailey wins the 100-metre gold medal at the Atlanta Olympics.

1997 Jean Chrétien's Liberal Party wins re-election in the federal election.

The "flood of the century" hits Manitoba's Red River valley, but "the big ditch" built many years earlier protects Winnipeg.

1998 An extraordinary ice storm devastates the Montreal region and eastern Ontario, destroying trees and leaving millions in cold and darkness as electrical systems collapse.

1999 Eaton's, a familiar name to Canadian shoppers for more than 100 years, goes out of business.

The new territory of Nunavut is established in Canada's eastern Arctic.

Adrienne Clarkson becomes Governor General of Canada.

2000 Canada enters a new millennium.

2001 Security alerts across Canada after terrorist attacks of September 11 on New York City and Washington.

2002 Canadian forces take up combat mission in Afghanistan.

Canada signs the Kyoto Accord, a global effort to reduce the greenhouse gases that cause global warming.

2003 Jean Chrétien retires as prime minister and is succeeded by Paul Martin.

SARS epidemic kills more than thirty people and causes fear in Toronto and Vancouver.

Hurricane Juan damages Halifax.

2004 The "Sponsorship Scandal" damages the reputation of the Liberal government.

CBC Television's "Greatest Canadian" contest chooses Tommy Douglas.

Same-sex marriages become legal throughout Canada.

2005 Canada sends aid to Asian countries devastated by New Year's Eve tsunami.

Michaëlle Jean becomes Governor General.

Canadian Steve Nash named National Basketball Association's Most Valuable Player.

2006 The Conservative party forms a minority government and Stephen Harper becomes prime minister of Canada.

"King Ralph" Klein retires after 14 years as premier of Alberta.

2007 Census results show Canada had 31, 612, 897 people in 2006.

Publishers' Acknowledgments

The publishers wish to acknowledge the financial support of the Canadian Studies and Special Projects Directorate of the Department of the Secretary of State of Canada.

Basil Johnston, O. Ont., of the Department of Ethnology of the Royal Ontario Museum read and commented upon an early draft of the manuscript. On numerous occasions, Jack Granatstein generously provided advice.

For kind permission to reprint material used herein, the publishers are grateful to: Farley Mowat, for the excerpt from *Never Cry Wolf*; and Ariel Rogers for the excerpt from the Stan Rogers song "Northwest Passage."

The excerpt from David Thompson's Narrative is taken from John Warkentin, ed., *The Western Interior of Canada: A Record of Geographical Discovery*, 1612–1917, Carleton Library No. 15 (Toronto and Montreal: McClelland and Stewart Limited, 1964, 1969), pp. 102-03. The passage from *Roughing It in the Bush*, by Susanna Moodie, is from the New Canadian Library edition, No. 31 (Toronto: McClelland and Stewart Limited, 1962, 1970), p. 194.

Authors' and Illustrator's Acknowledgments

Malcolm Lester and Louise Dennys first suggested this book to us, and we began it with the support of the editorial team they assembled at Lester & Orpen Dennys, particularly Carol Martin and Sandra LaFortune. We completed it with the help of Kathy Lowinger at Lester Publishing and Phyllis Bruce and her staff at Key Porter Books, who handled a thousand last-minute details and guided the manuscript through to publication.

The authors wish to thank the Ontario Arts Council for a grant that helped them to complete the work. We also thank the staffs of the public libraries of Trenton and Kitchener, Ontario, and of the Metropolitan Toronto Central Reference Library, as well as many writers, readers, and friends who listened well.

The illustrator would like to thank the staff of the Kitchener Public Library, especially those in the Grace Schmidt Room. Staff at many other institutions were enormously helpful: at the Canadian Museum of Civilization, Dr. Bryan C. Gordon, Dr. David Keenlyside, and their fellow curators; at Parks Canada, Richard Lindo and René Chartrand; at Fort Edmonton Park, Jane Repp; at the National Aviation Museum, Rénald Fortier. I received assistance from the archives of the CPR; Fort Ticonderoga, N.Y.; Ste-Marie Among the Hurons; Historic Naval and Military Establishments at Penetanguishene; the Citadel, Halifax; the Royal Ontario Museum (Sigmund Samuel Collection); and from most of the provincial archives.

I would also like to express my appreciation to Commander Tony German, RCN (Ret.), and to the late J. Merle Smith, my father-in-law, who inspired me with his love for historical illustrations.

Picture Credits

All the illustrations in the book are by Alan Daniel, with the exception of those credited below. The following abbreviations have been used:

AGO: Art Gallery of Ontario, Toronto
AO: Archives of Ontario, Toronto
CP: Canapress Photo Service
CTA: City of Toronto Archives/James Collection
CW: Canada wide
CWM: Canadian War Museum
FL: First Light Associated Photographers
GA: Glenbow Archives, Calgary
ISTC: Industry, Science and Technology Canada
MTL: Metropolitan Toronto Reference Library, Toronto
MTL/JRR: ———/John Ross Robertson Collection
NAC: National Archives of Canada
NASA: National Aeronautics and Space Administration
NGC: National Gallery of Canada, Ottawa
PAA: Provincial Archives of Alberta

Front
Page i: AO/6520 S13458; iii: NGC/© Ozias Leduc 1992/VIS*ART.

Chapter One
Page 2: GA/NA2676-6; 3, top: CWM/CN8567; bottom: NAC/PA-568; 4: Dept. of National Defence/NAC/PA-1020; 5: Robert Semeniuk/FL; 6, top: NAC/PA-1654; bottom: Kitchener Public Library; 7, top: MTL/JRR/Ephemera Collection; bottom: CTA/#640; 8: top: NAC/PA-1892; bottom: Janet Lunn; 9: NAC/C-95266; 10, right: CTA/#2451; 11, top: MTL/T31725; bottom: Manitoba Provincial Archives/Foote Collection; 12, top: Canada's Sports Hall of Fame/NAC/PA-50440; bottom: General Motors of Canada Ltd.; 14: AGO/Gift of the Canadian Club of Toronto, 1926; 16 City of Edmonton Archives; 17: H. Wright Corp./NAC/PA-142372; 18: GA/NA-1831-1; 19, top: AO/S801; bottom: PAA/A5145; 20, top: Canadian Government Motion Picture Bureau/NAC/C-80917; bottom: CTA/#2040; 21: Canada Post; 22, top: Claude Detloff/NAC/C-38723; bottom: Montreal Gazette/NAC/PA-129617; 23, top and bottom: MTL/JRR/Ephemera Collection; 24: CWM/CN12276; 25: AGO/Study Collection/T-1340; 26: CWM/CN11356; 27: NAC/C-52832; 28: York University Archives, Toronto Telegram Photographic Collection; 29: NAC/PA-117812; 30 top: NAC/C-261110; bottom: CWM/CN14085; 31: Tak Toyota/NAC/C-46350; 33, right: NAC/PA-136280; 34, left and right: NAC/Comics; 34: W.J. Hynes/Dept. of National Defence/NAC/PA-147114.

Chapter Two
Page 39: National Aviation Museum; 40: Farley Mowat; 41: NGC/(c) Estate of William Kurelek, permission granted by the Isaacs/Innuit Gallery of Toronto; 42, top: Canada's Sports Hall of Fame; bottom: CP; 43: National Film Board of Canada/NAC/PA-128080; 44: Duncan Cameron/NAC/C-94168; 45: Montreal star/NAC/PA-129625; 46: NAC/PA-143954; 47, top: CP; bottom: CP; 48: Ford Motor

Company of Canada Ltd.; 49: CP; 50: Stratford Festival Archives; 51, top: Robert Semeniuk/FL; bottom: CP; 52: CW; 53, top: CP; bottom: Indian and Northern Affairs Canada; 54: Leo Harrison/CW; 55: Daggett/Montreal Star/NAC/PA-139982; 57, top left: T.G.A. Henstridge/NAC/Heraldry (3); bottom left: J. Evariste-Alain/NAC/Heraldry (2); top right: NAC/Heraldry (15); middle right: Osy-Mandias/NAC/Heraldry (7); bottom right: Germain Tremblay/NAC/Heraldry (12); 60: NAC/C-30085; 61: Peter Bregg/CP; 62: F. Lenon/The Toronto Star; 63: Doug Ball/CP; 64: ISTC; 65: Buston/CP; 66: Glen Ross/New Brunswick Power; 67, top right: K. Dykstra/FL; bottom left: Karl Sommerer; 68, top: reprinted by permission of Macmillan Canada; bottom: from The Olden Days Coat by Margaret Laurence, used by permission of the Canadian Publishers, McClelland & Stewart, Toronto; 69: NASA; 70: CP; 71: Jim Russell/FL; 72: top: Tom Hanson/CP; bottom left: 73: Vellis Crooks/CP; 74: NASA; 75: Jacques Nadeau/CP; 76: Peter McLeod/FL; 77: top: Jacques Boissinot/CP; bottom right: Hans Deryk/CP; 78: Shaney Komulainen/CP; 79: William C. Stratas; 80: Paul Chiasson/CP; 81: Tom Hanson/CP; 82: Ryan Remiorz/CP; 83: Wayne Cuddington/CP; 84: Tom Hanson/CP; 72: Harry Foster/CWM; 86: Ryan Remiorz/CP; 88: Tom Hanson/CP; 89: Sophie Giraud/CBC; 90: Ruth Bonneville/CP; 91: Fred Chartrand/CP.

Northern Voyagers
Page 85, top: Mike Beedell; bottom: CP; 86-87: Paul von Baich/FL.